I0474403

Real World

Colouring Book

For Advanced Users & Adults

50 Images

Created From Real Life Photos
For You To Colour As You Please.

ISBN 978-0-359-86479-9
90000
9 780359 864799

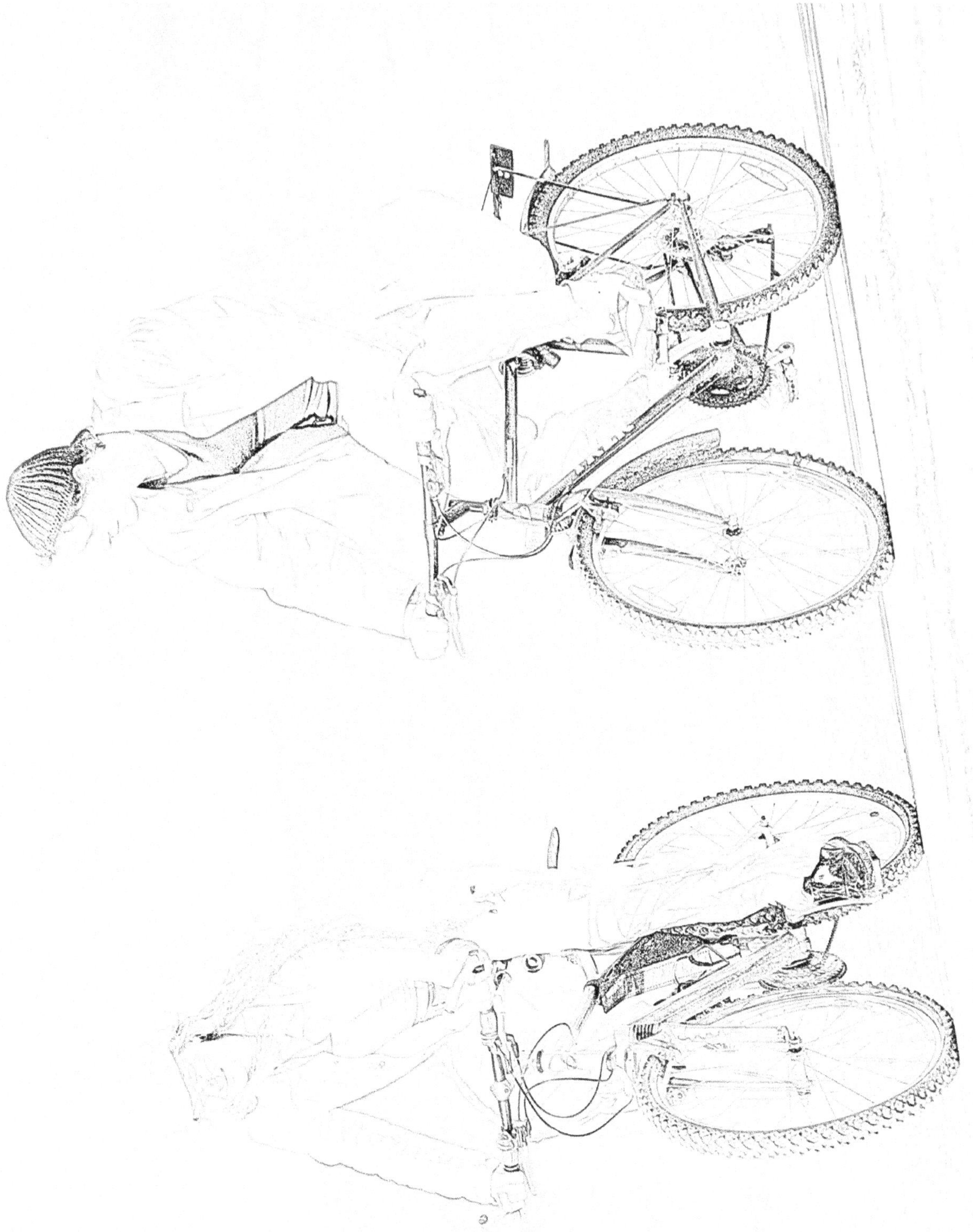

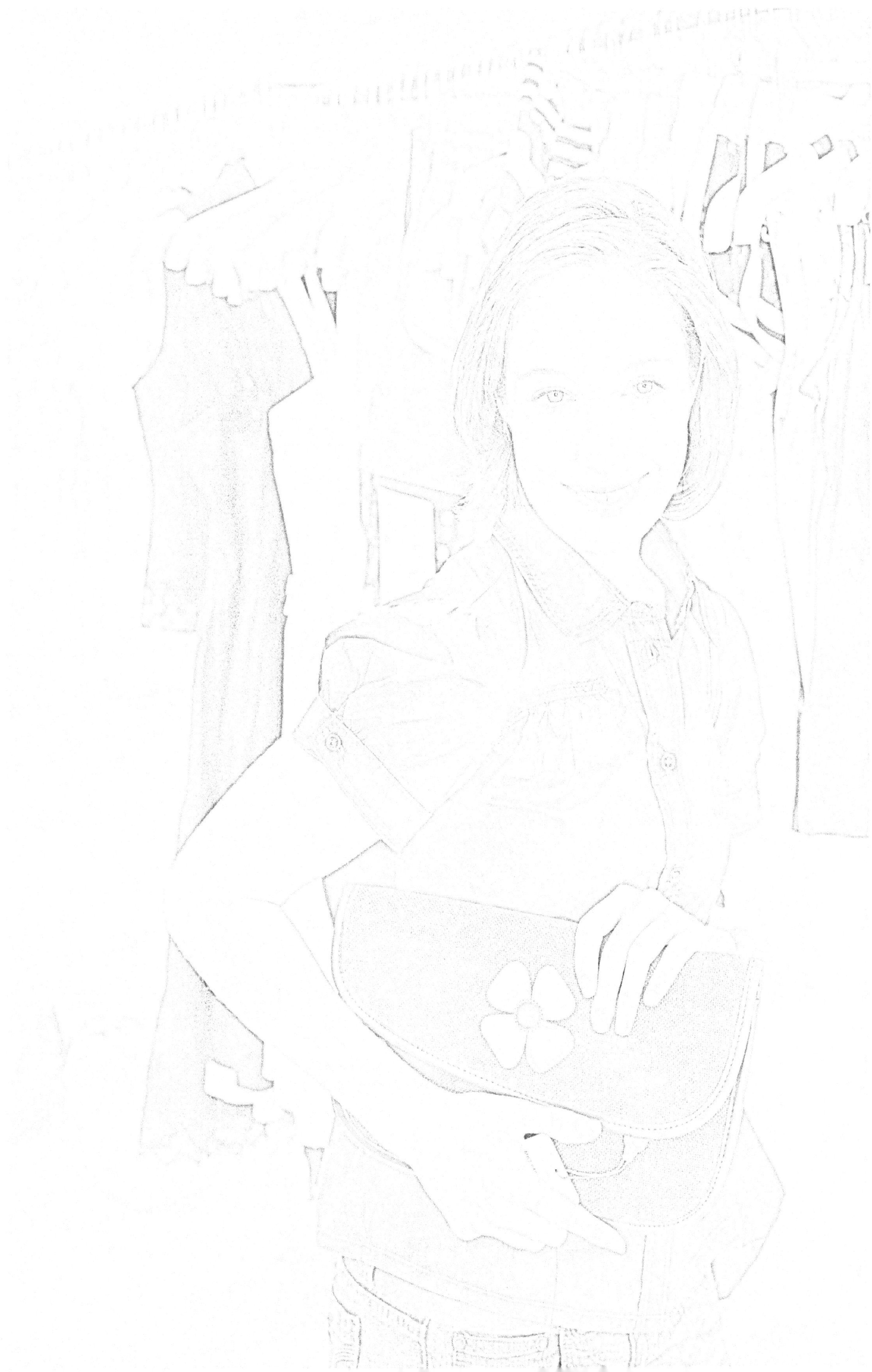

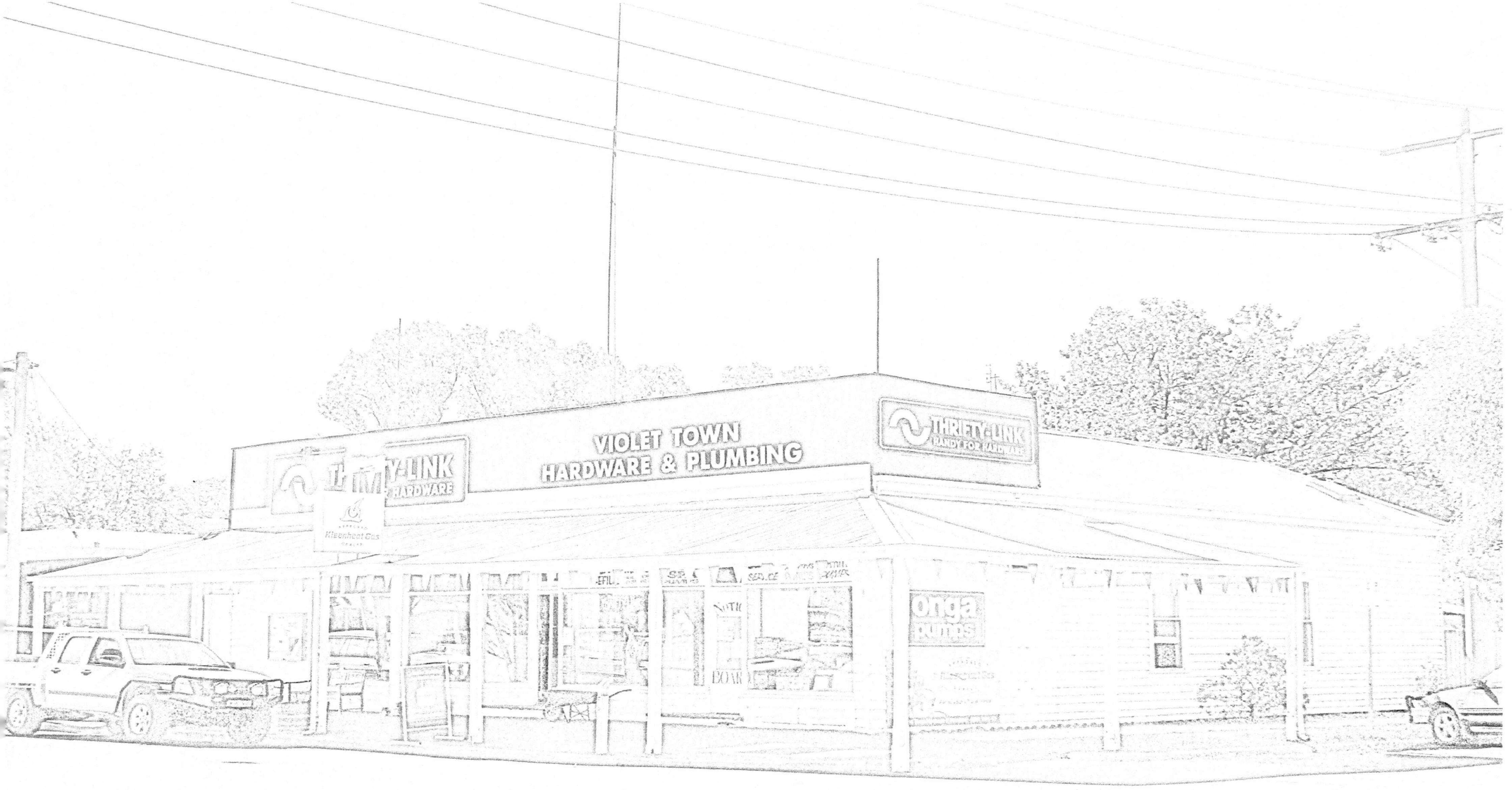
VIOLET TOWN
HARDWARE & PLUMBING
THRIFTY-LINK
THRIFTY-LINK
HARDWARE
Kleenheat Gas
Onga
pumps

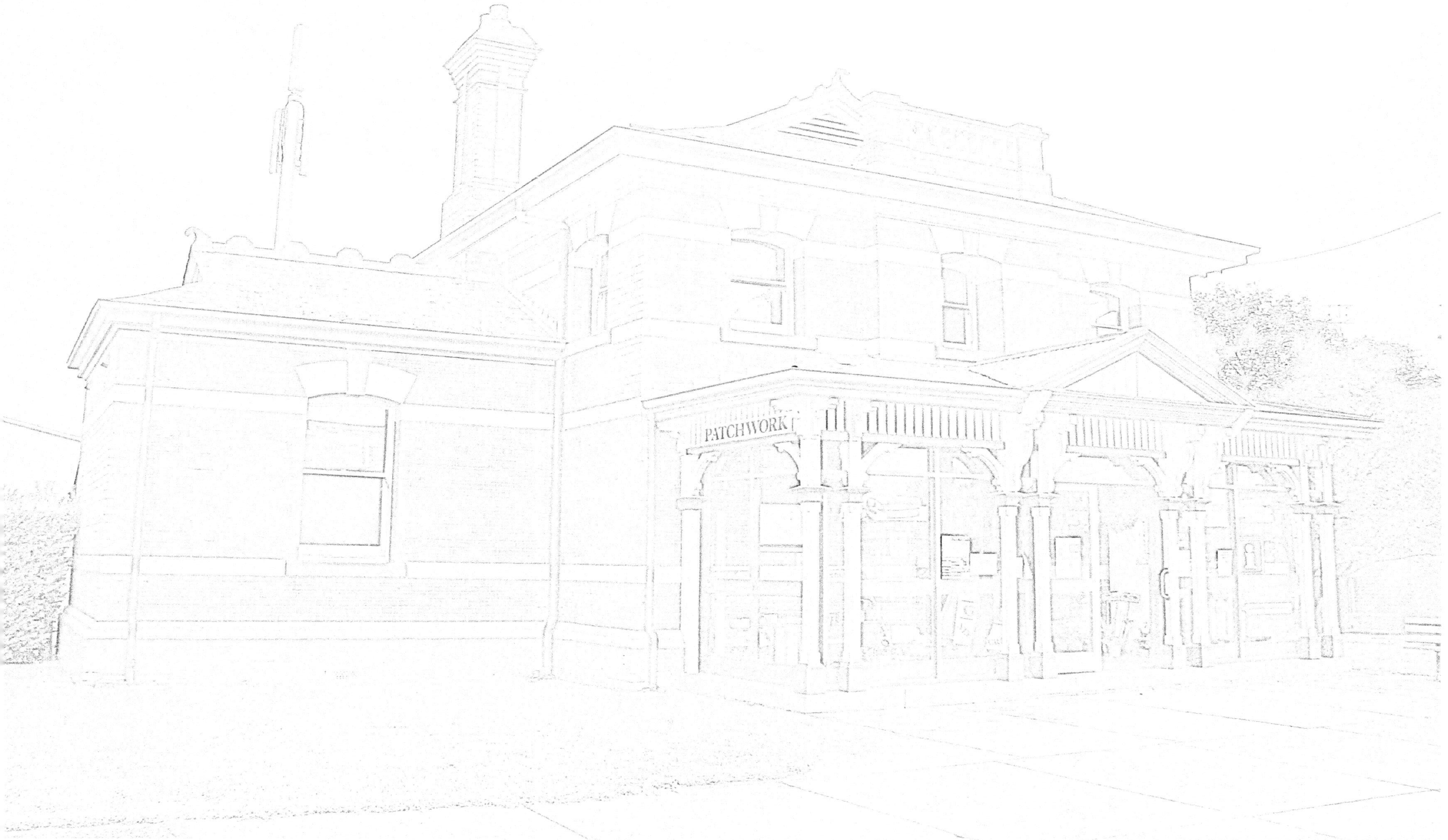
PATCHWORK

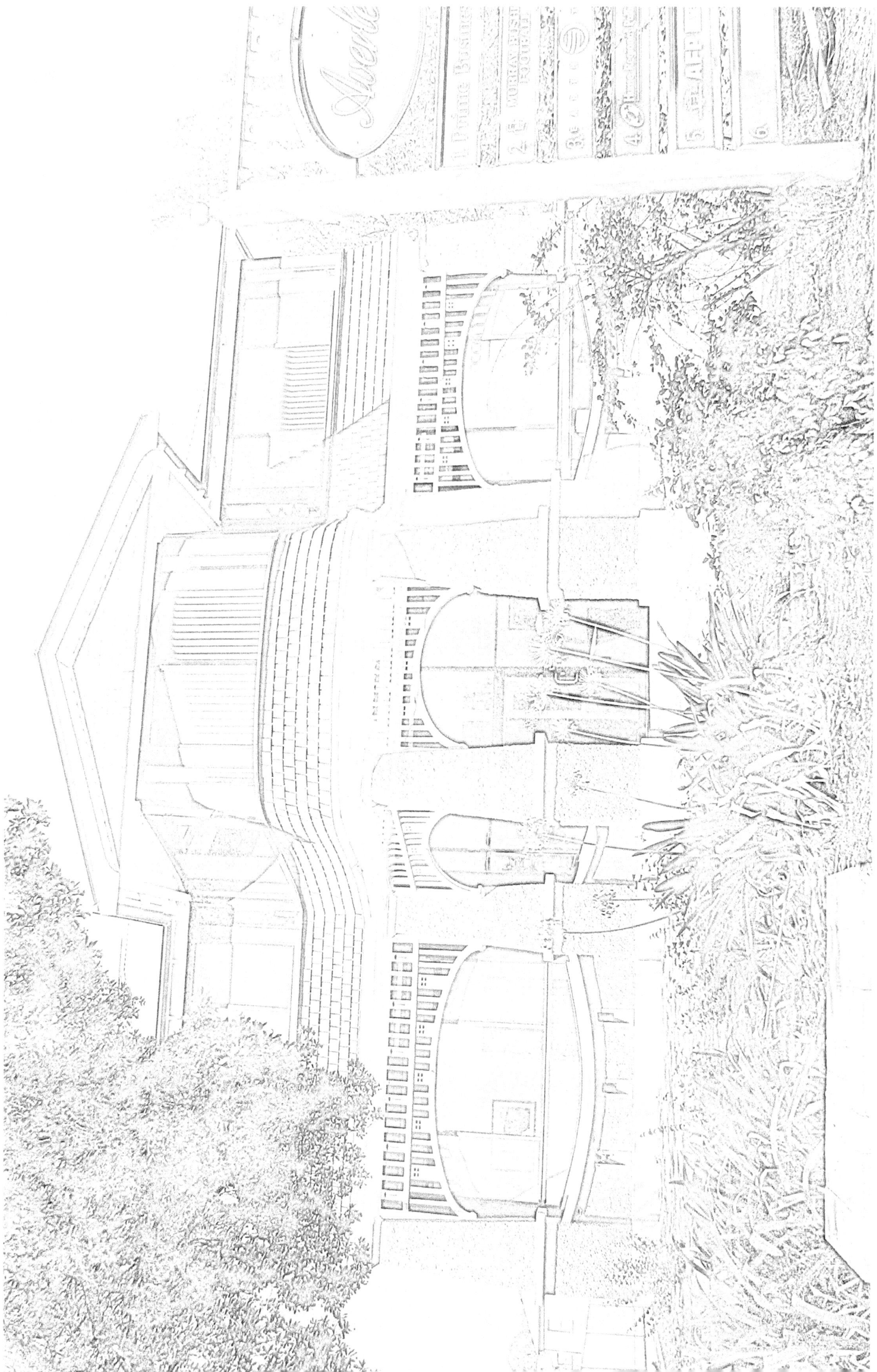

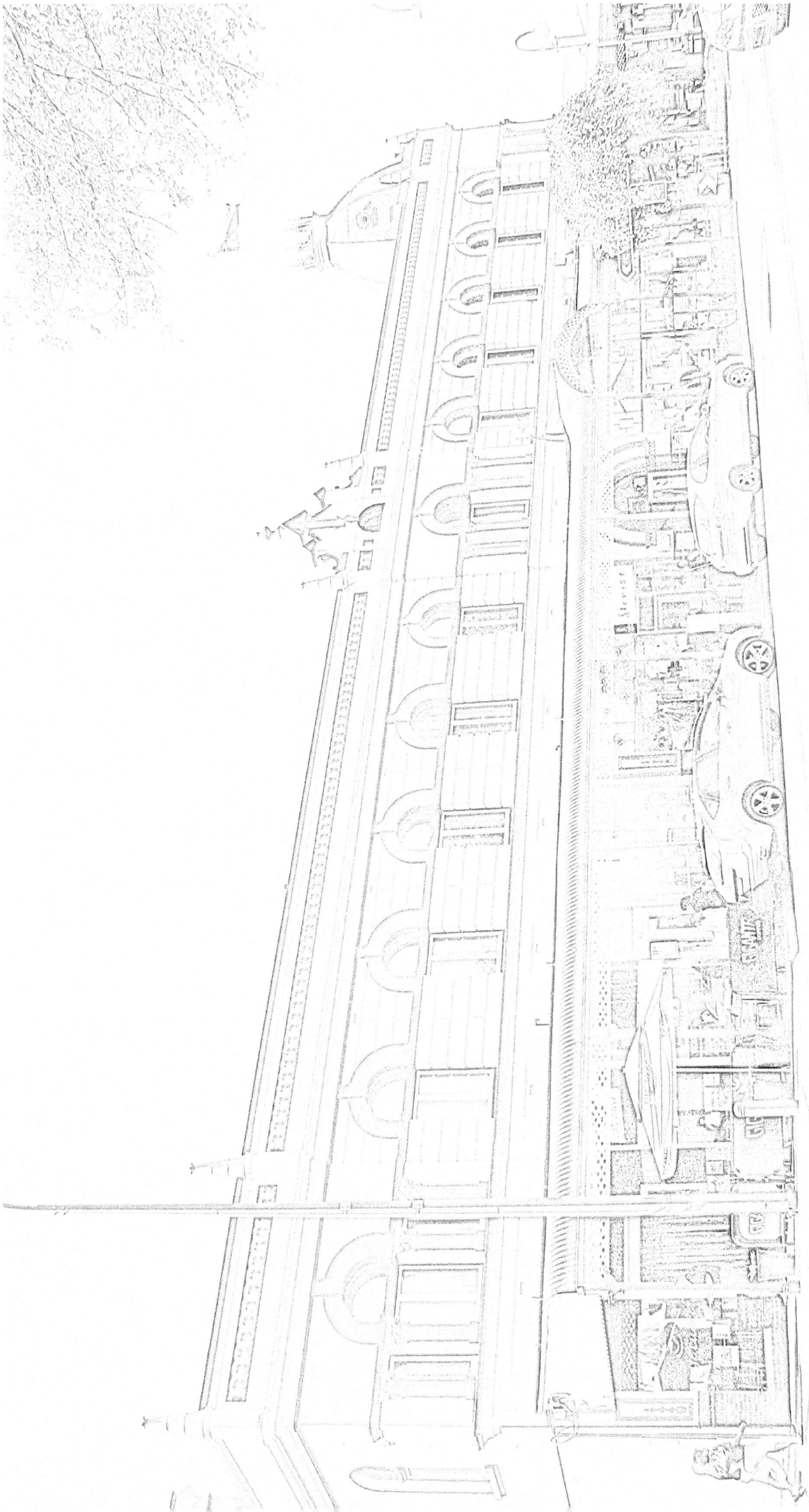

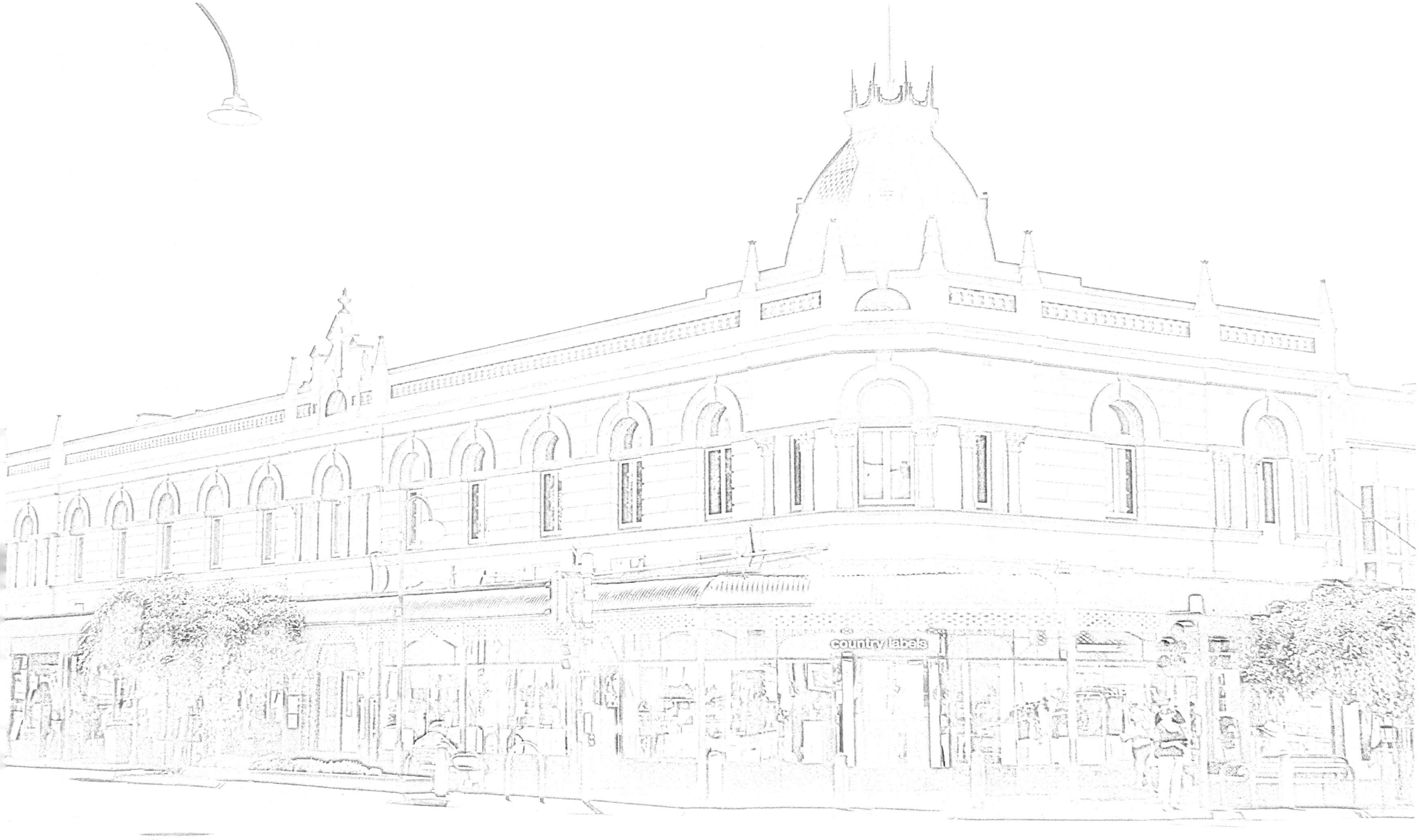
country labels

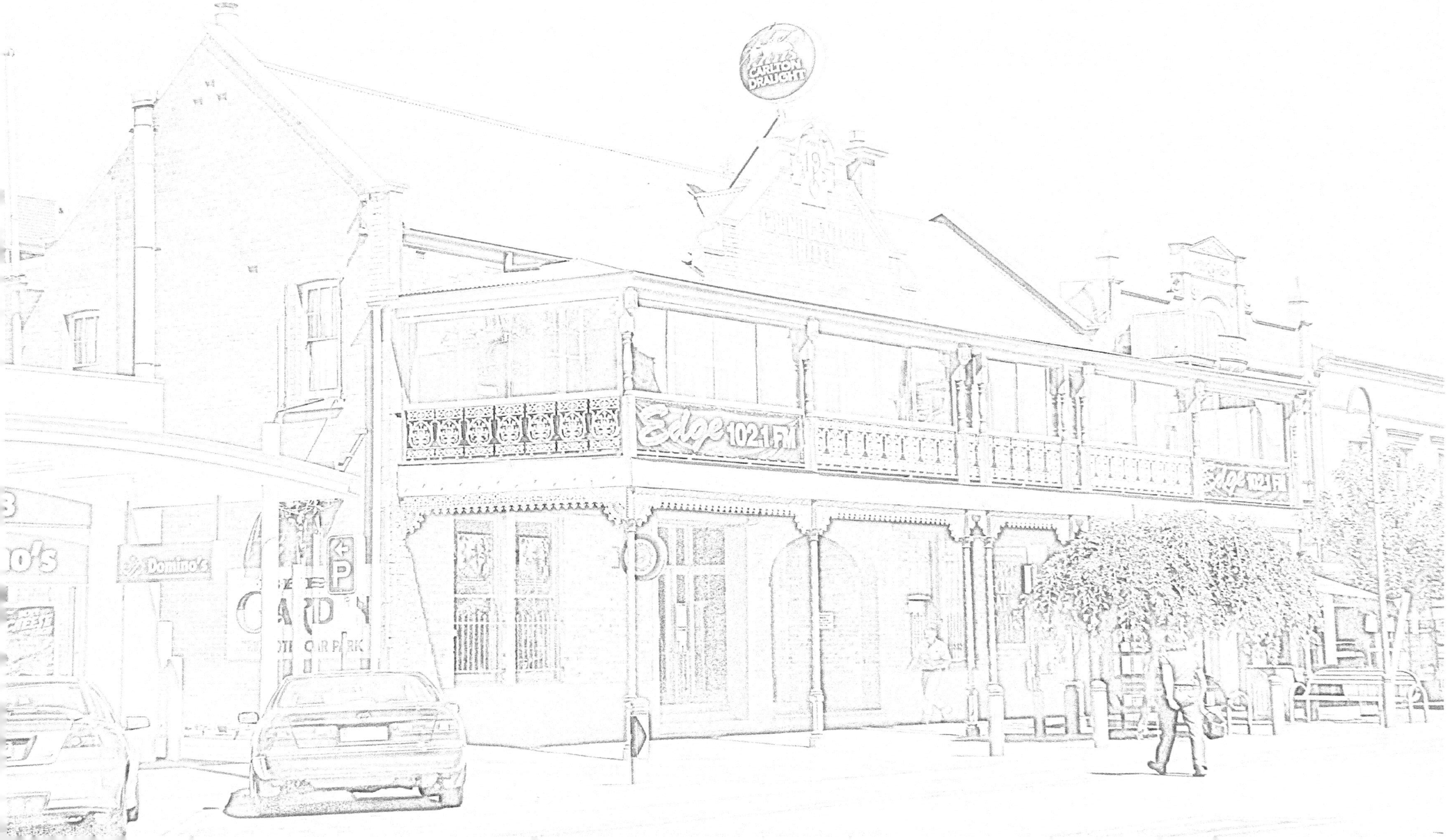
CARLTON DRAUGHT
Edge 102.1 FM
Domino's
P
CAR PARK

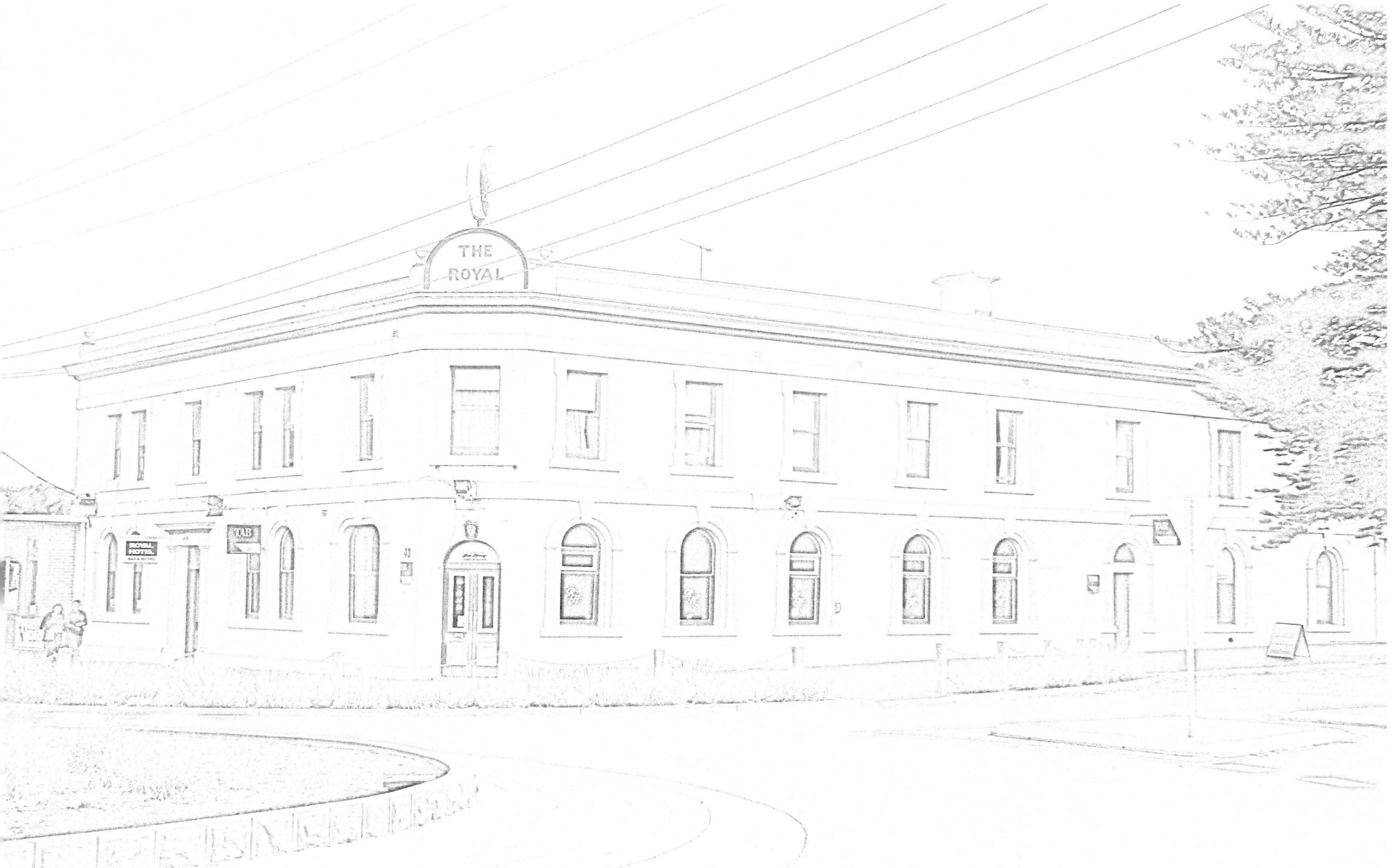
THE ROYAL
TAB
ROYAL HOTEL
43

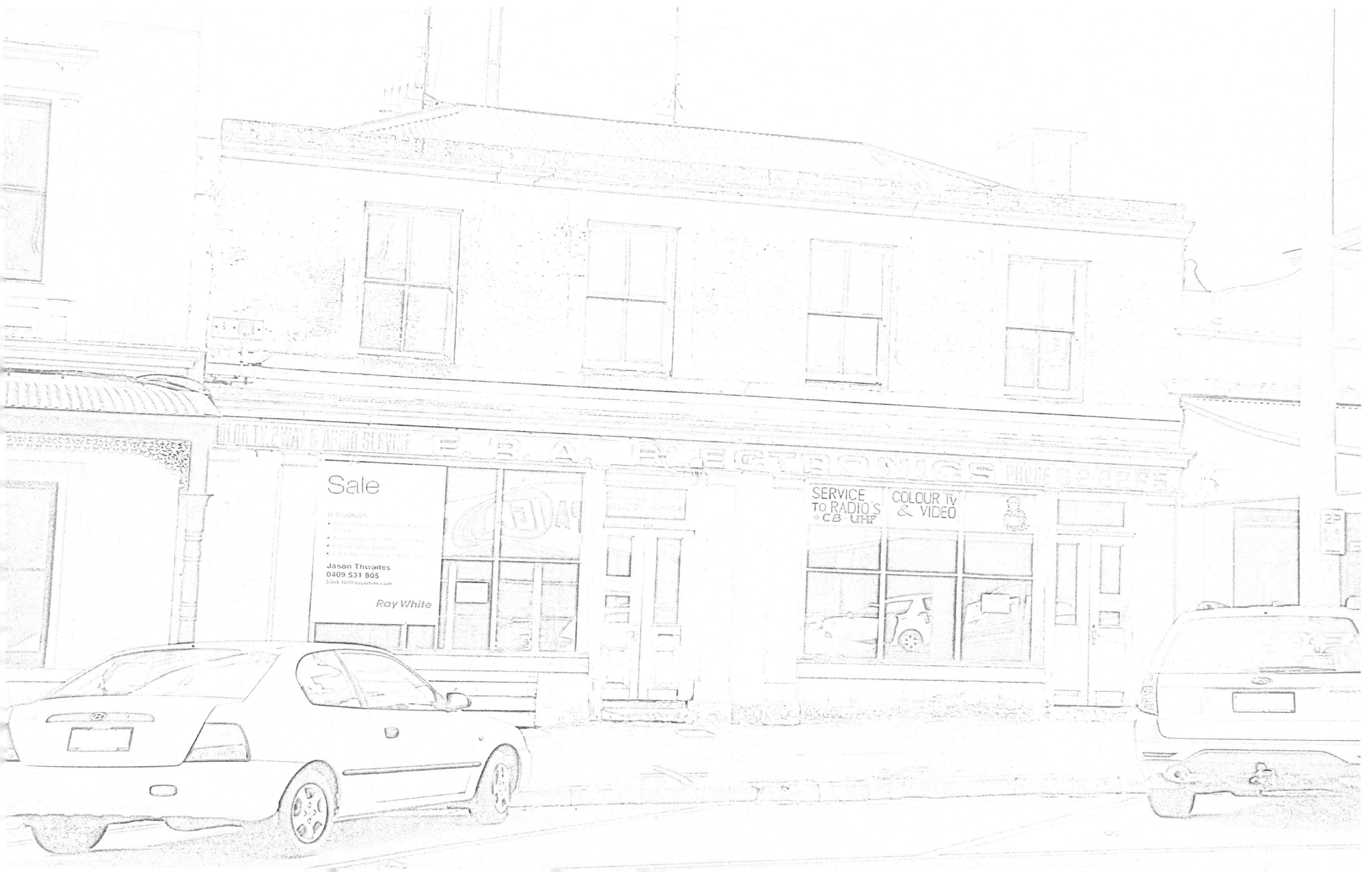
Sale
Jason Thwaites
0409 531 805
Ray White
SERVICE
TO RADIO'S
CB UHF
COLOUR TV
& VIDEO
2P

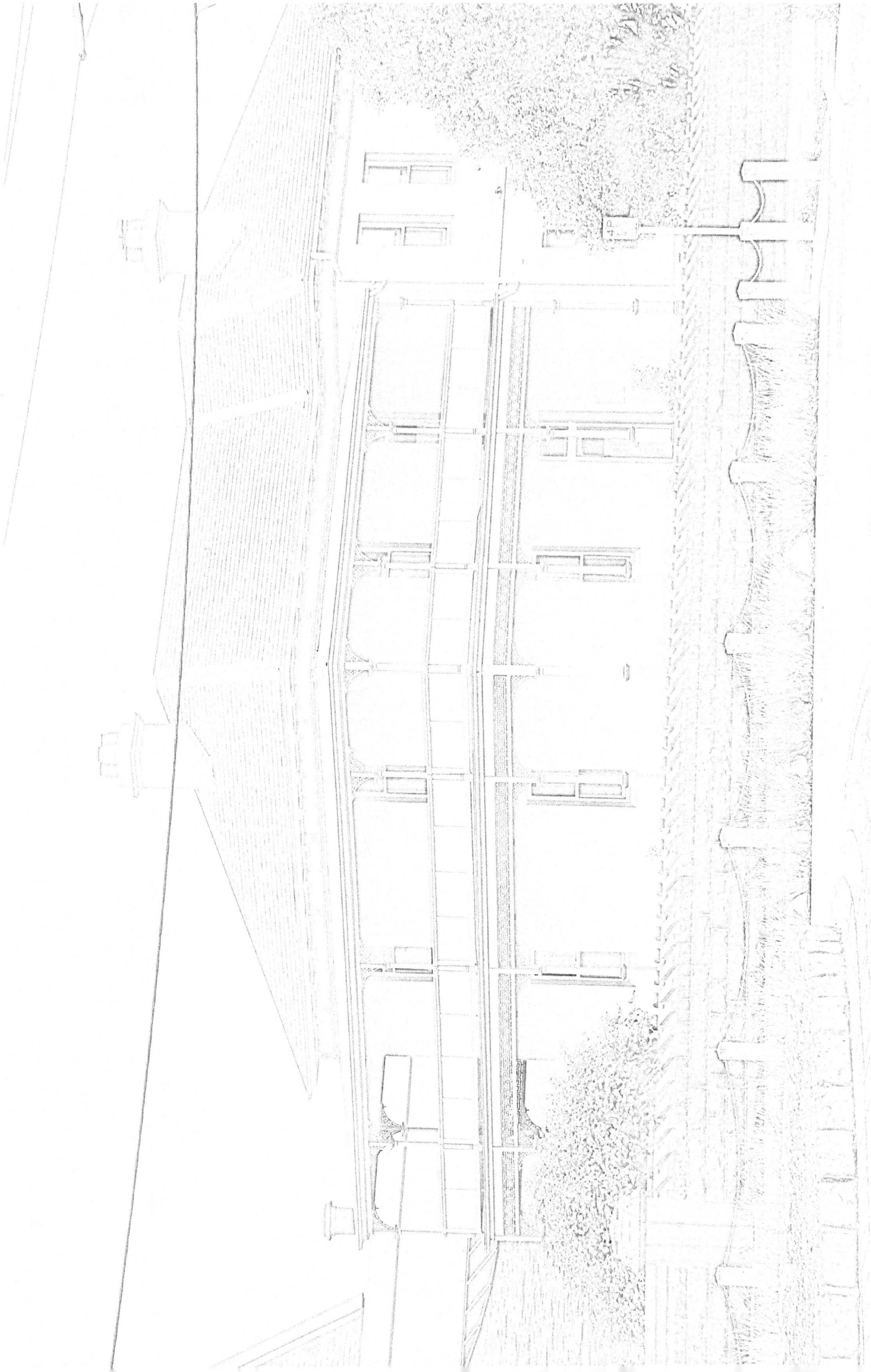

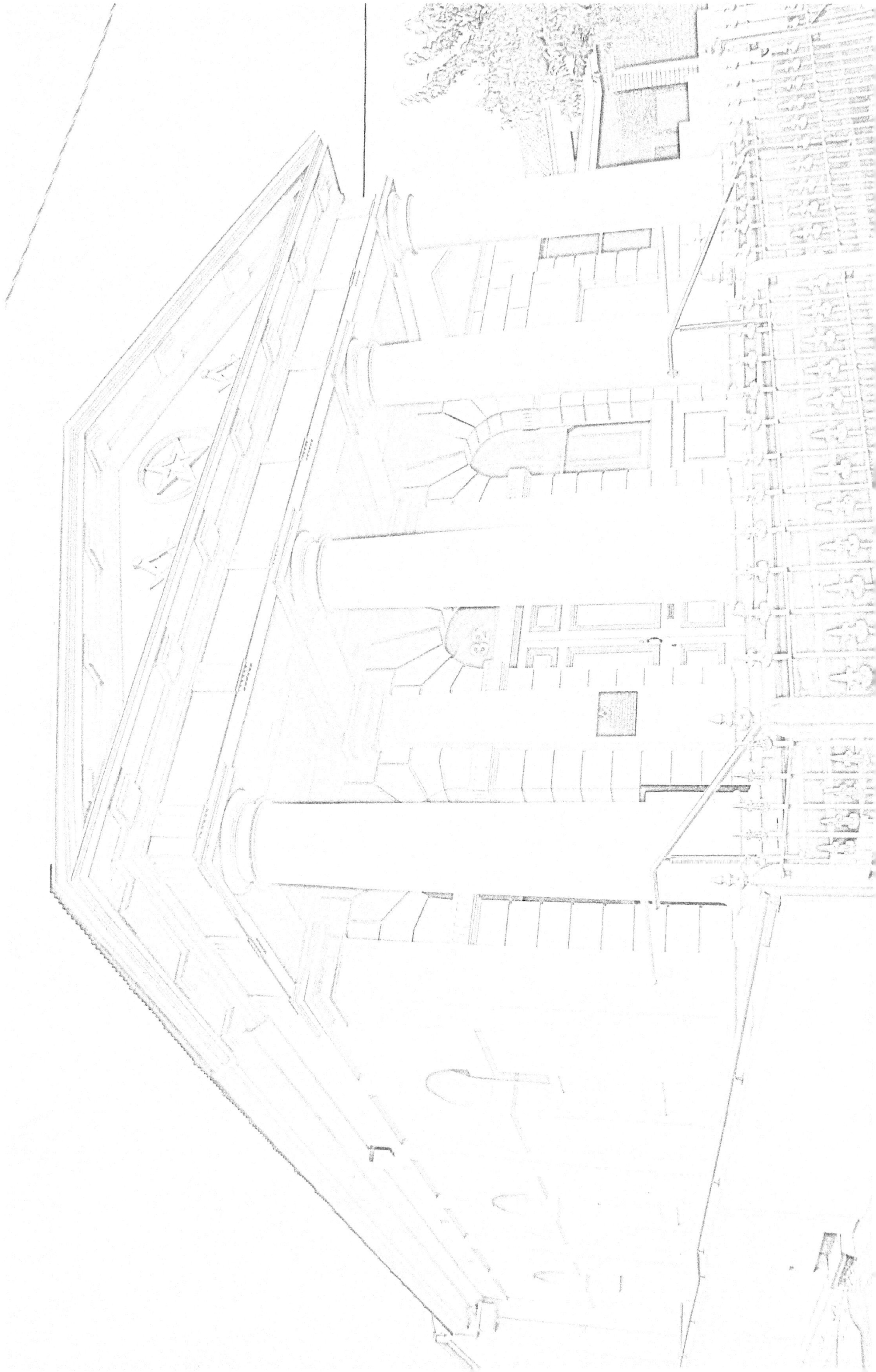

$1 coin
5 10 15 20 25 30 35 40 45 50 55 60 65 70 75 80 85 90 95 100 105 110 115 120 125

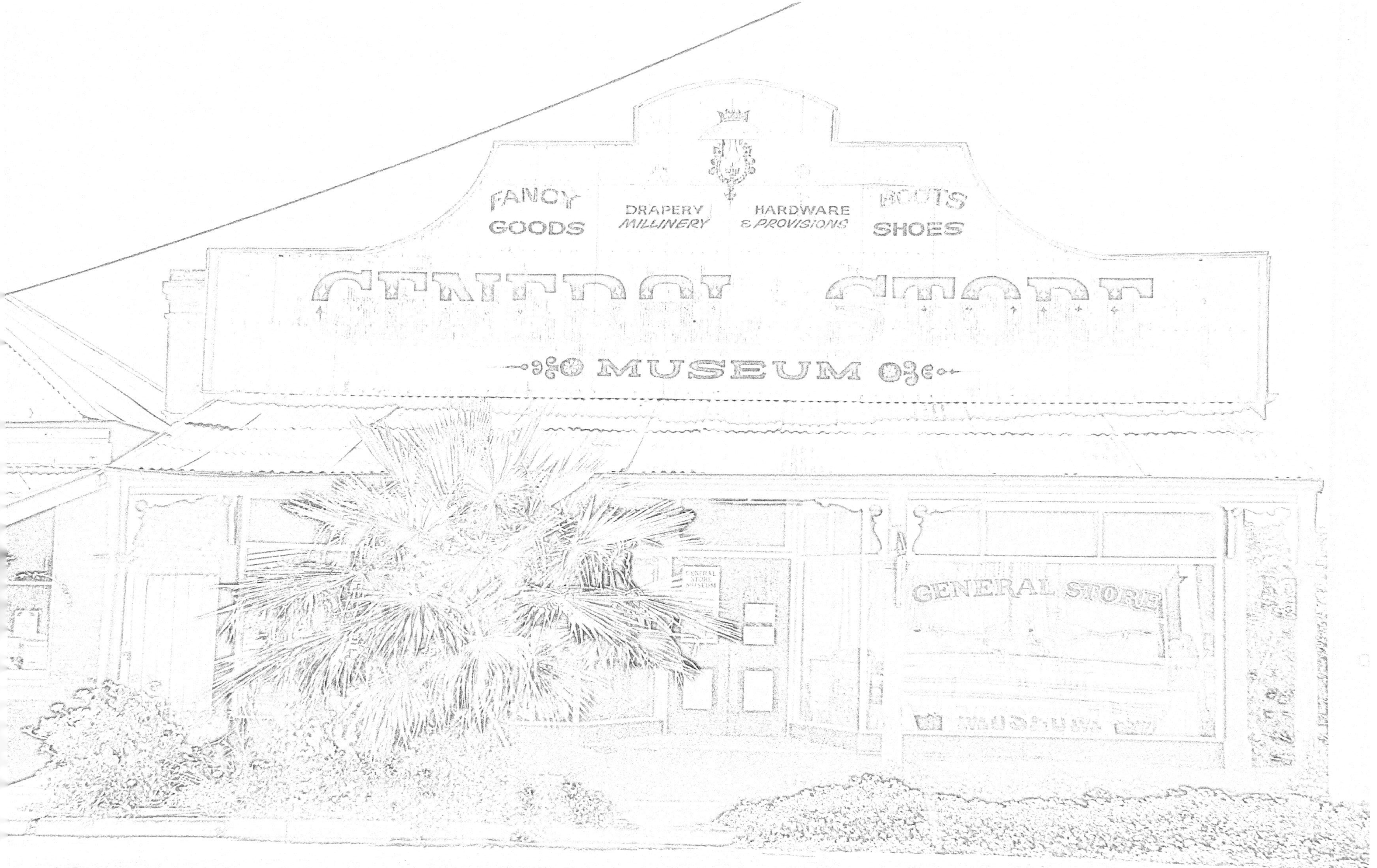
FANCY
GOODS
DRAPERY
MILLINERY
HARDWARE
& PROVISIONS
BOOTS
SHOES
MUSEUM
GENERAL STORE

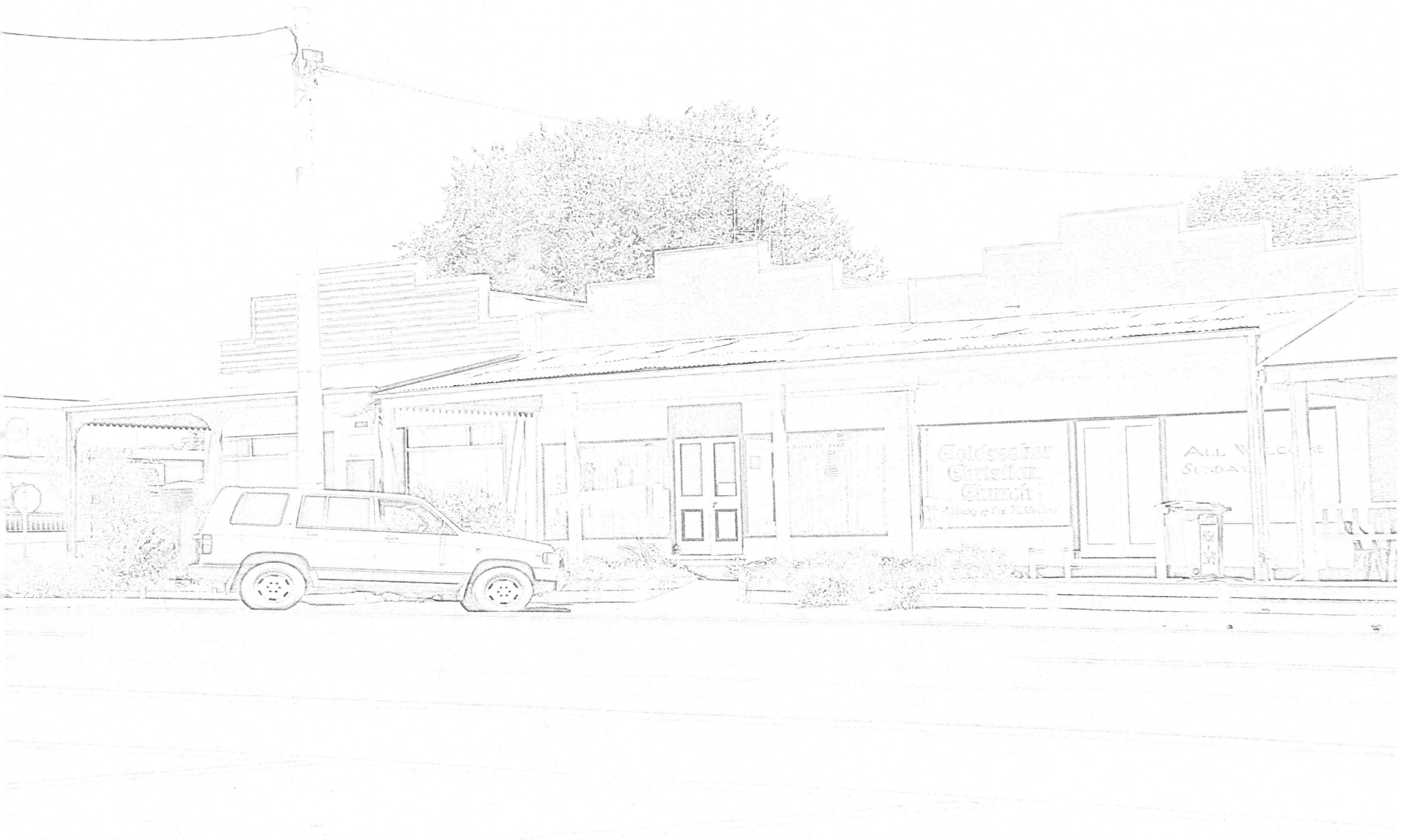
Goldseeker
Christian
Church

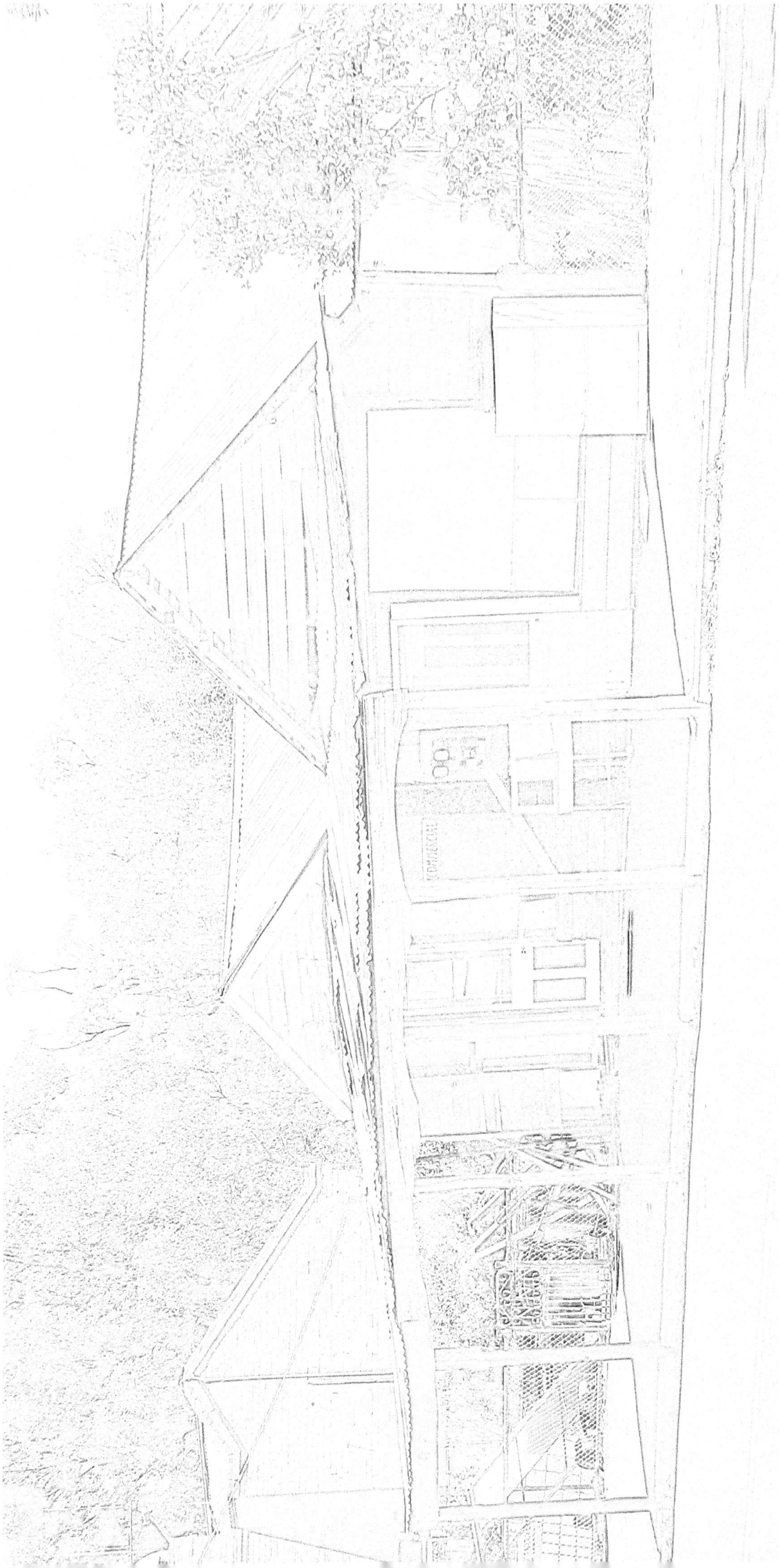

STATION ST
QUALITY
MEATS
BUTCHERS
1P
ONLY
PORK
BEEF
POULTRY
9741 2735
LAMB
FIS
22 STATION ST
Pork this good
deserves its own Festival

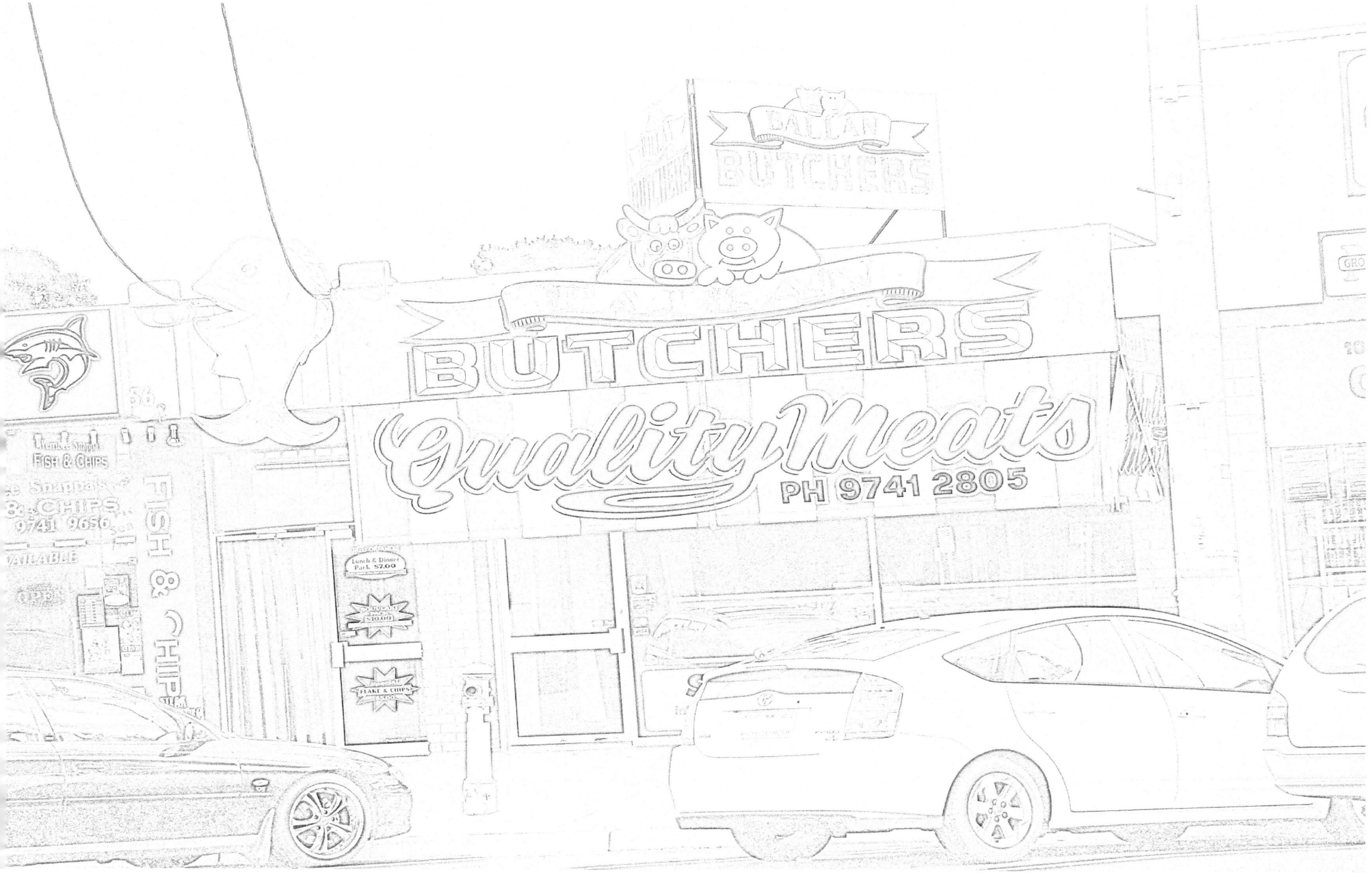
BALLAN
BUTCHERS
BUTCHERS
Quality Meats
PH 9741 2805
FISH & CHIPS
Lunch & Dinner Pack $7.00
$10.00
FLAKE & CHIPS

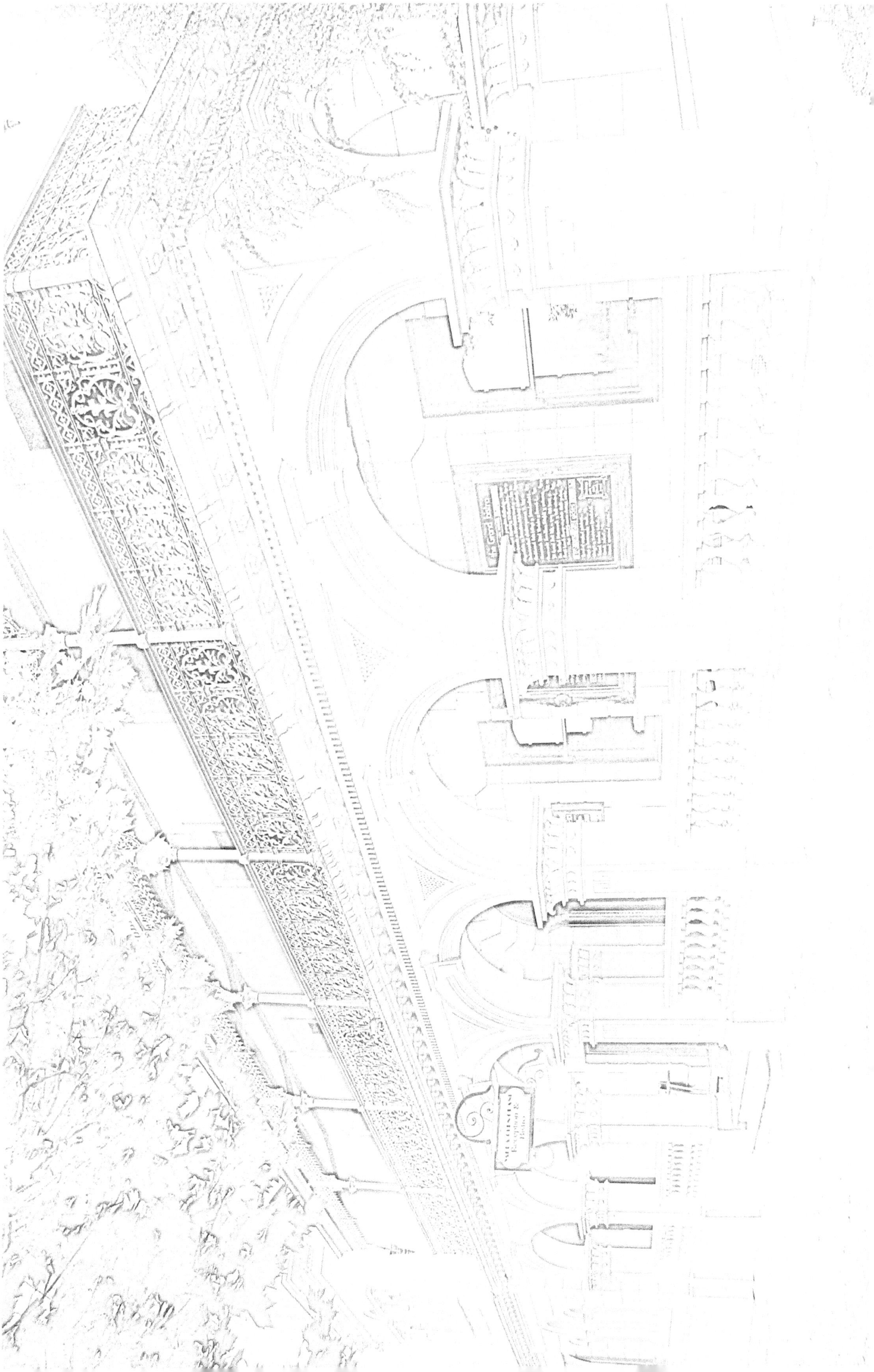

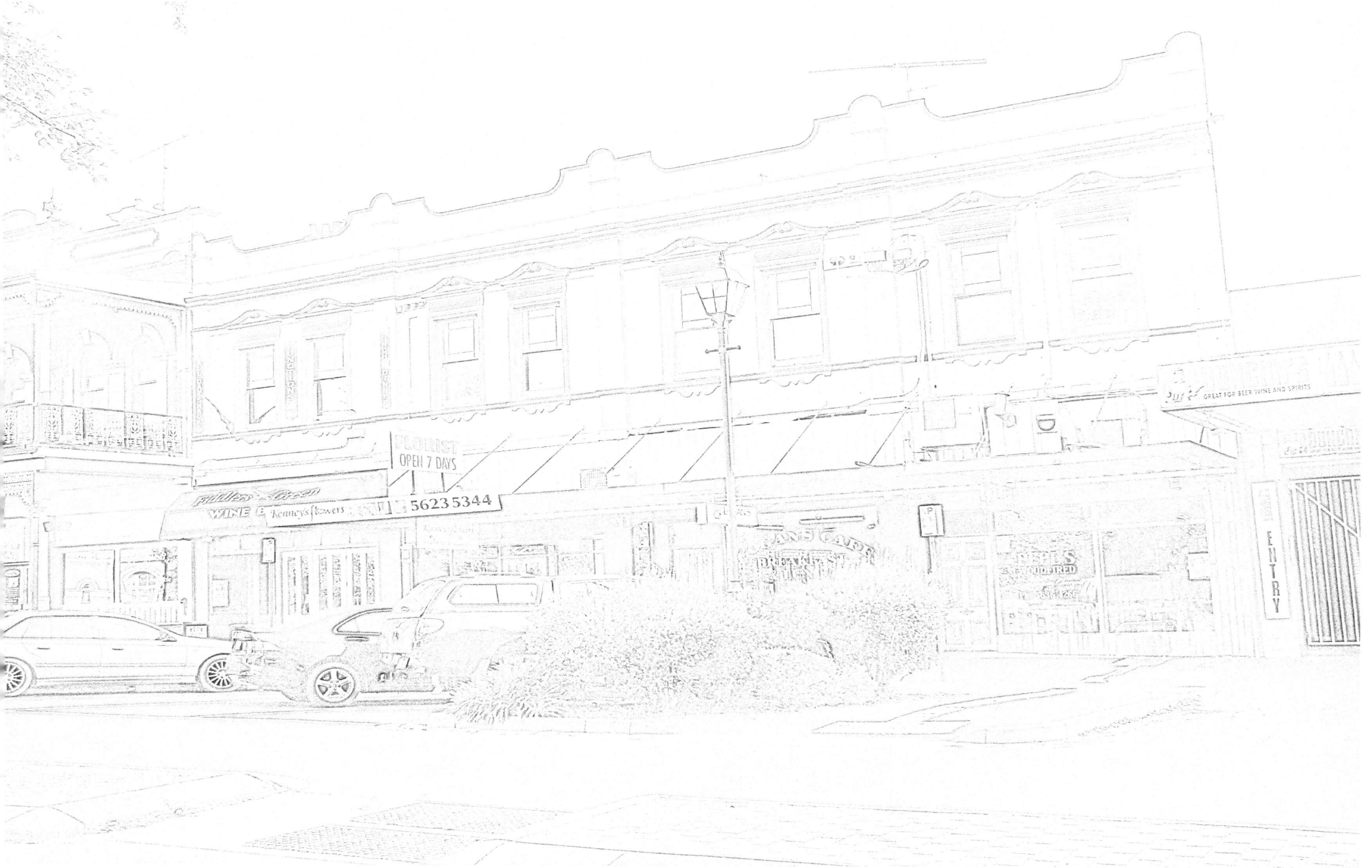

FLORIST
OPEN 7 DAYS
5623 5344
Fiddlers Green
WINE
Kenneys flowers
BREAKFAST
GREAT FOR BEER WINE AND SPIRITS
ENTRY

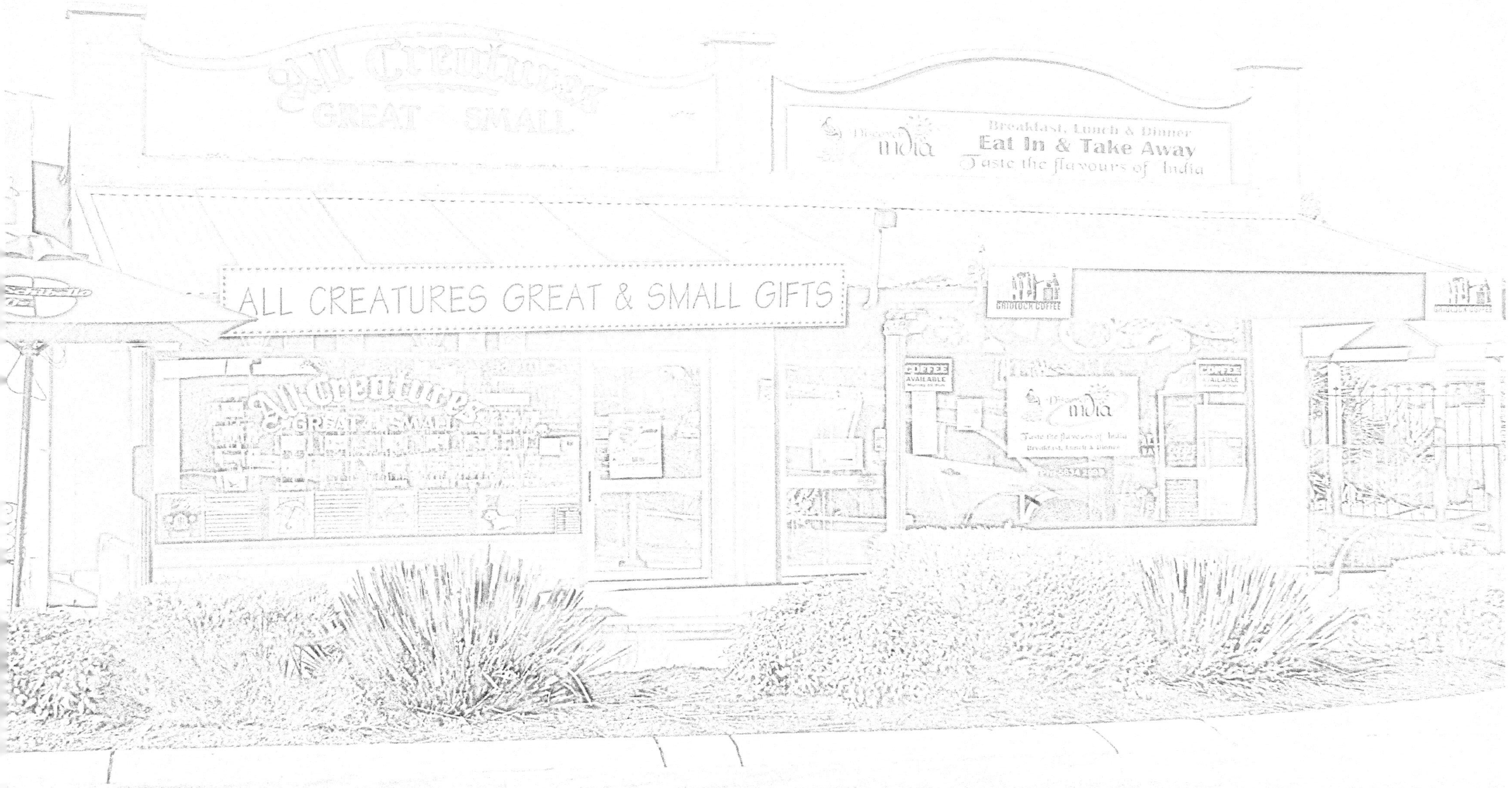
All Creatures
GREAT SMALL
ALL CREATURES GREAT & SMALL GIFTS
Discover India
Breakfast, Lunch & Dinner
Eat In & Take Away
Taste the flavours of India
GRIDLOCK COFFEE
AVAILABLE

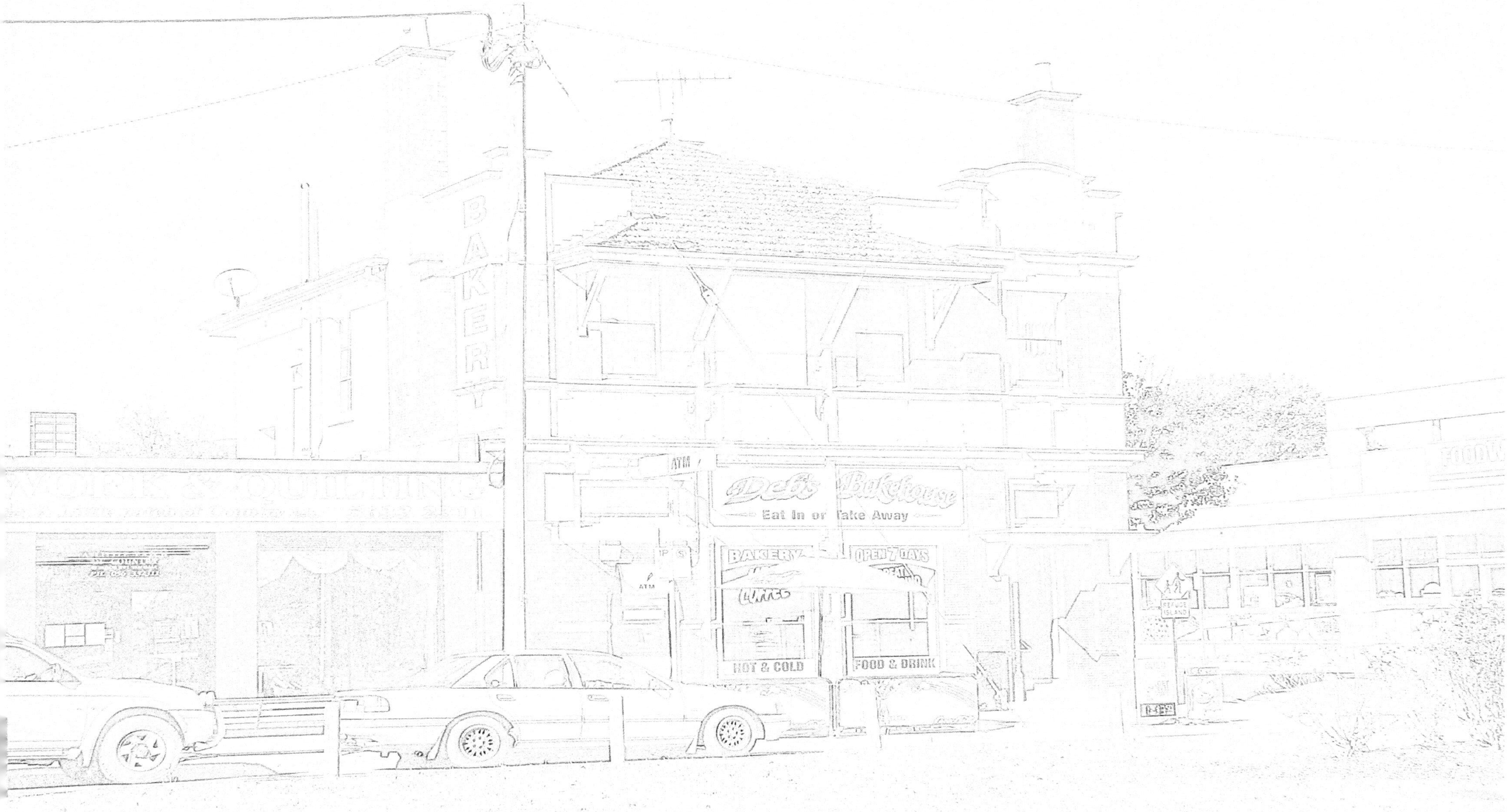
BAKERY
Deb's Bakehouse
Eat In or Take Away
ATM
BAKERY
OPEN 7 DAYS
HOT & COLD
FOOD & DRINK
REFUGE ISLAND

WALHALLA
GOLDFIELDS RAILWAY
VICTORIA'S MOST SPECTACULAR RAILWAY

STAWELL POST OFFICE
POST
GUIDE to STAWELL
20

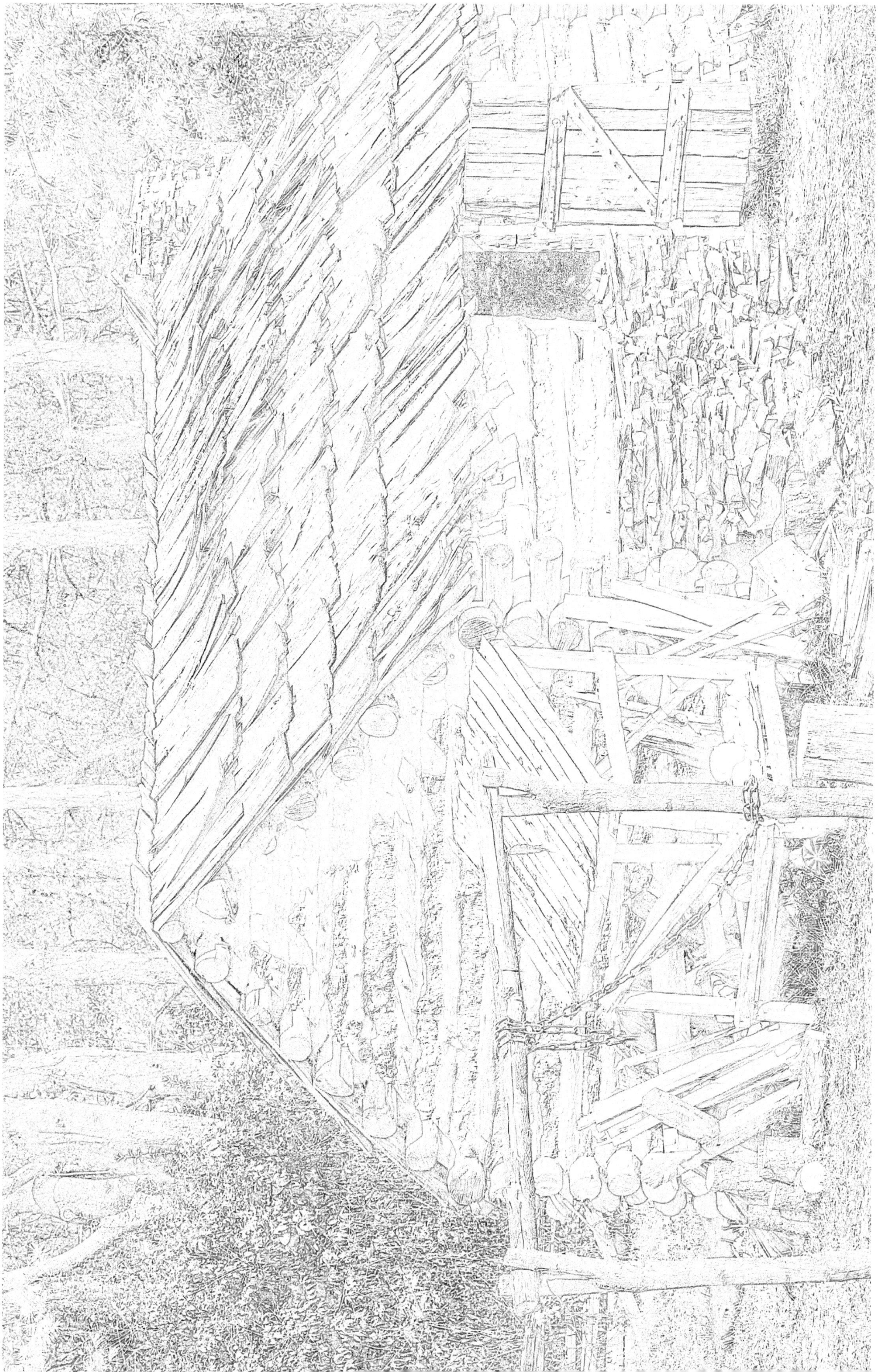

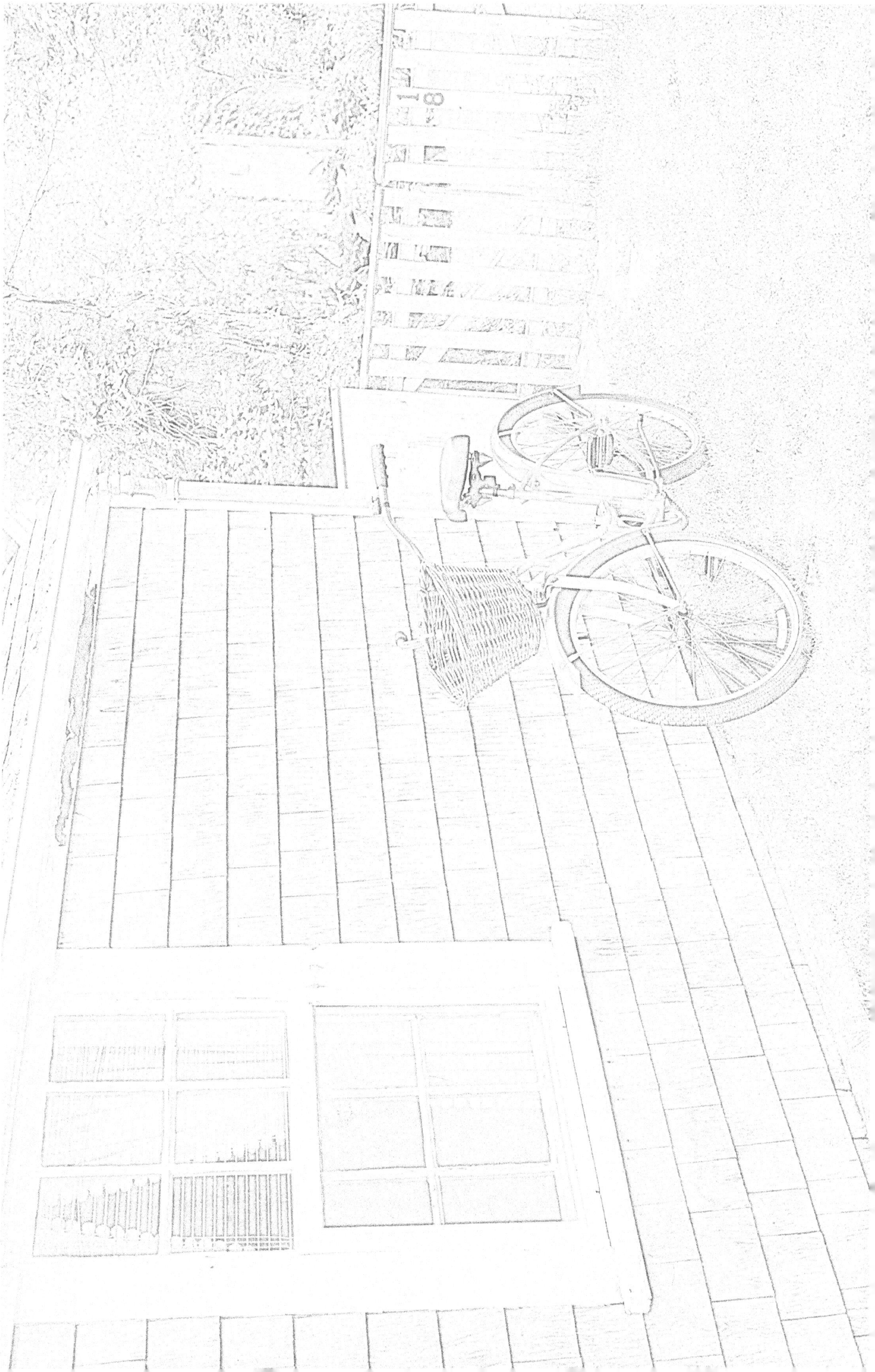

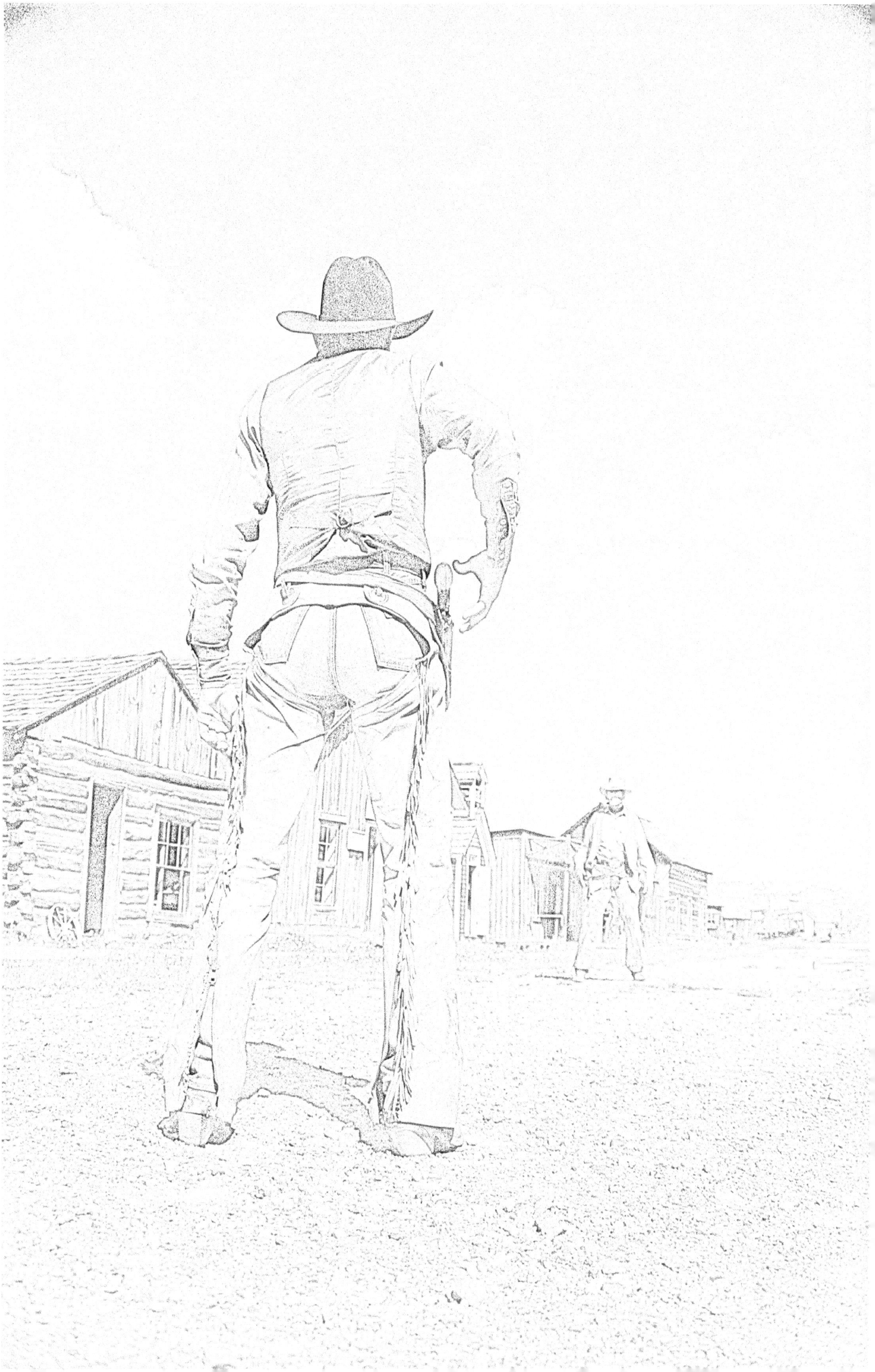

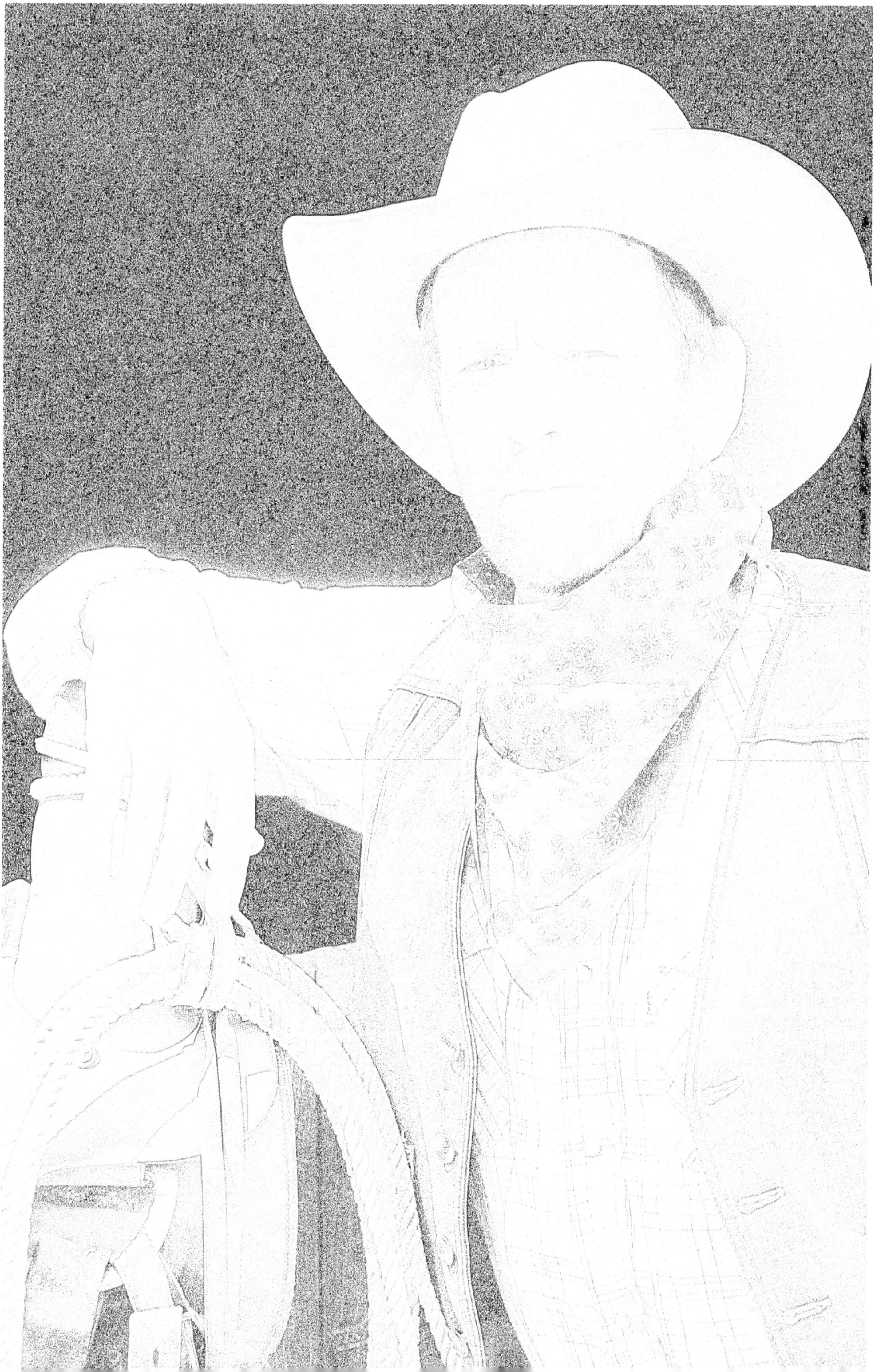

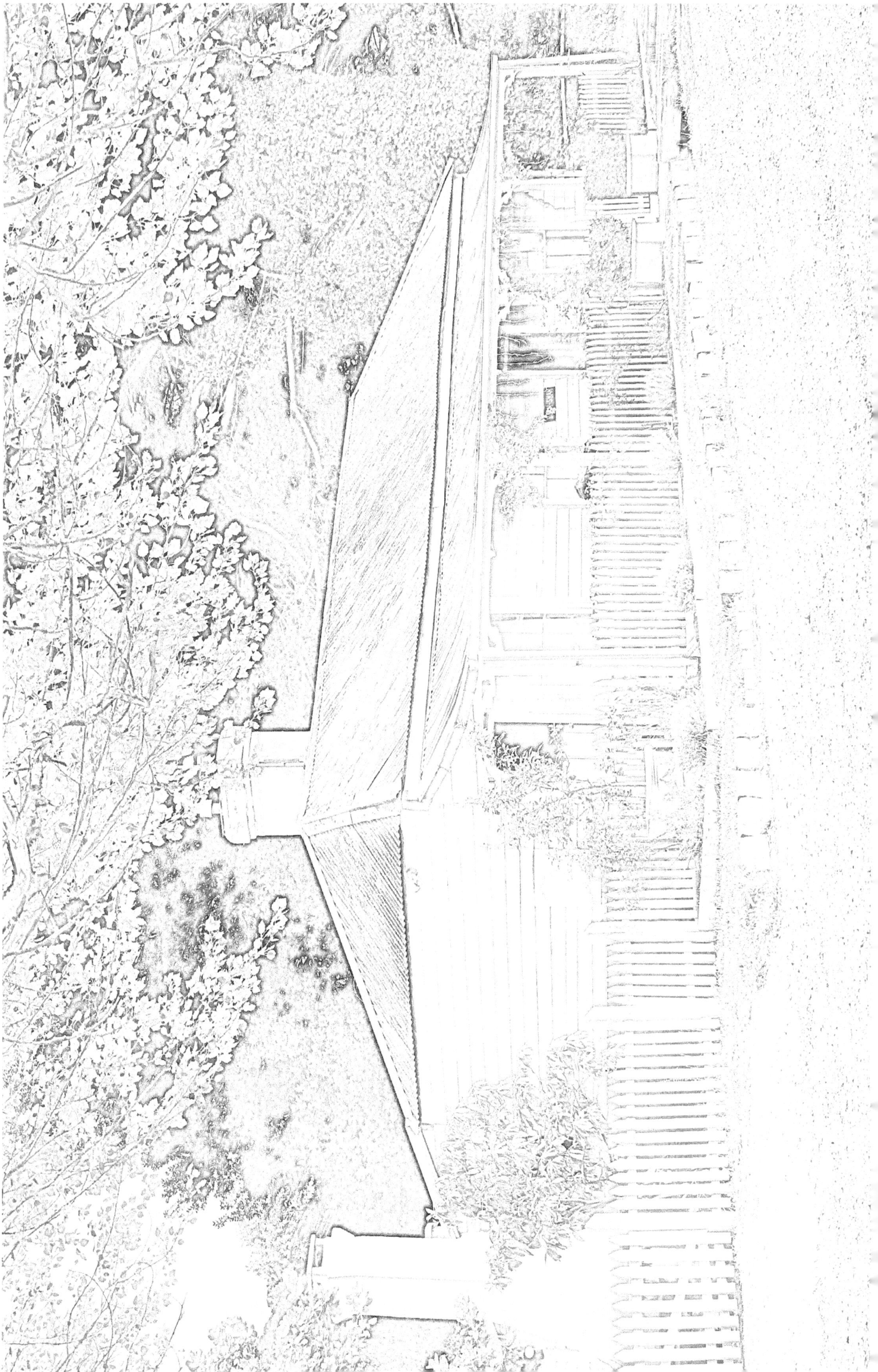

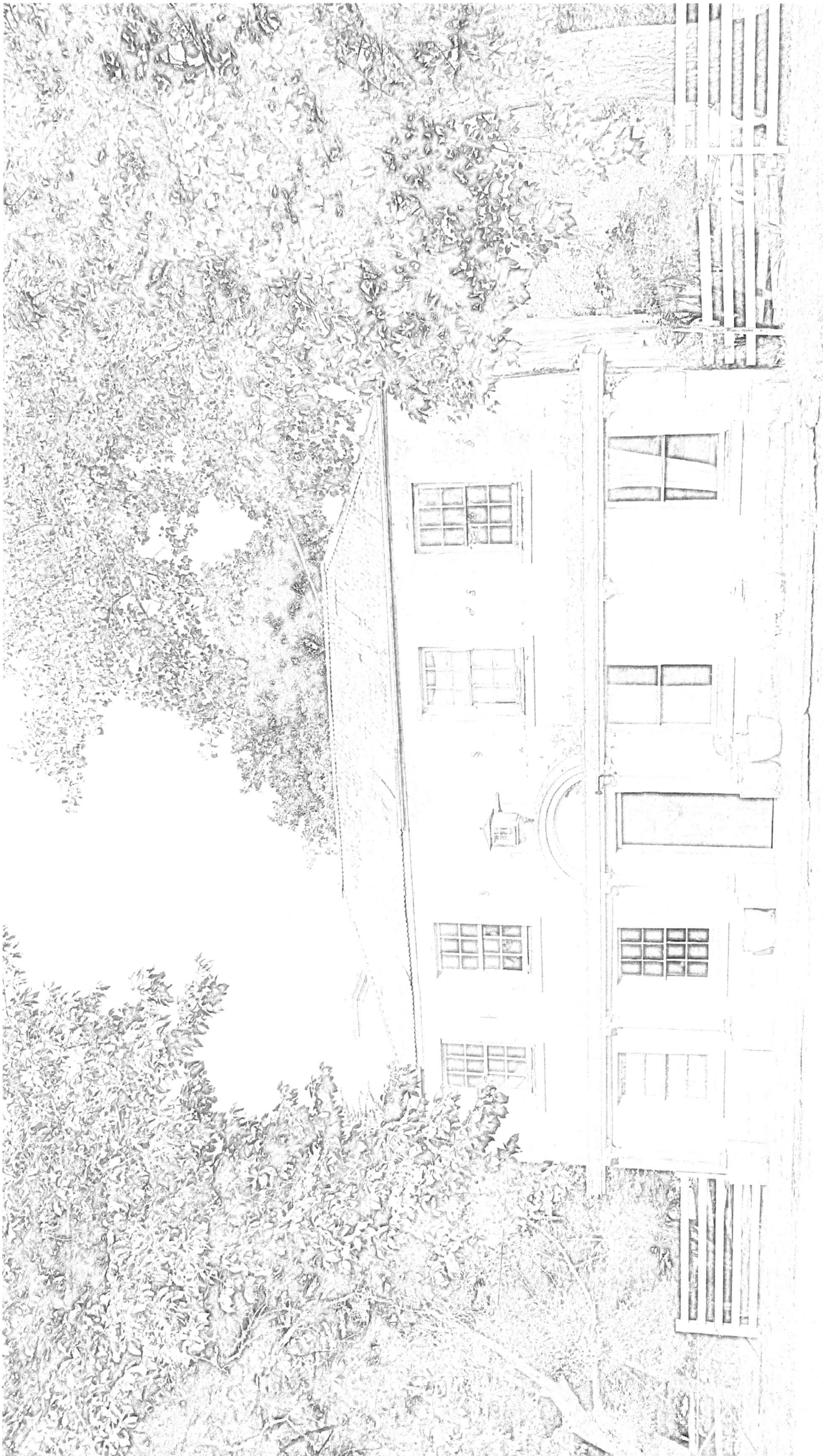

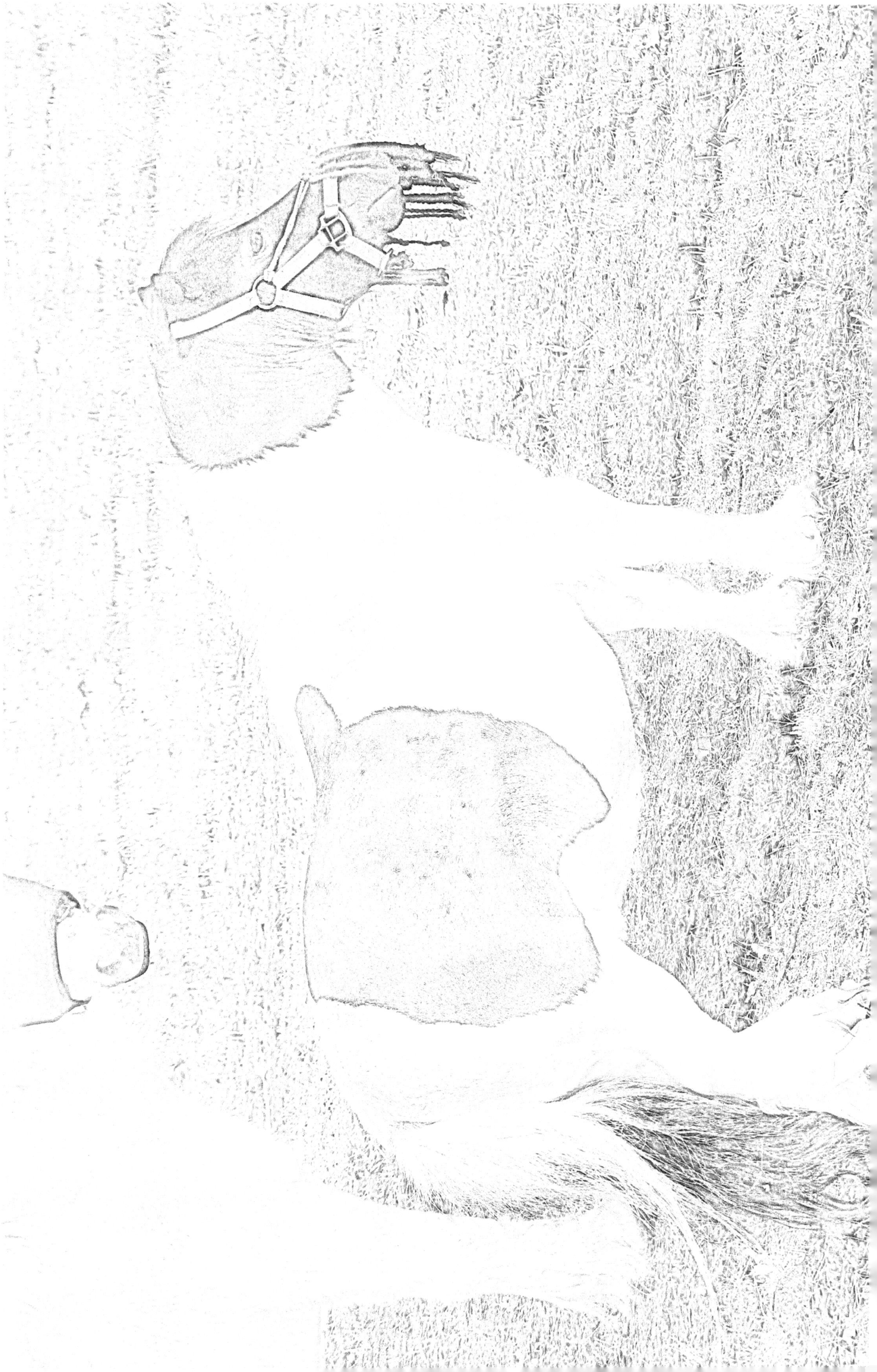

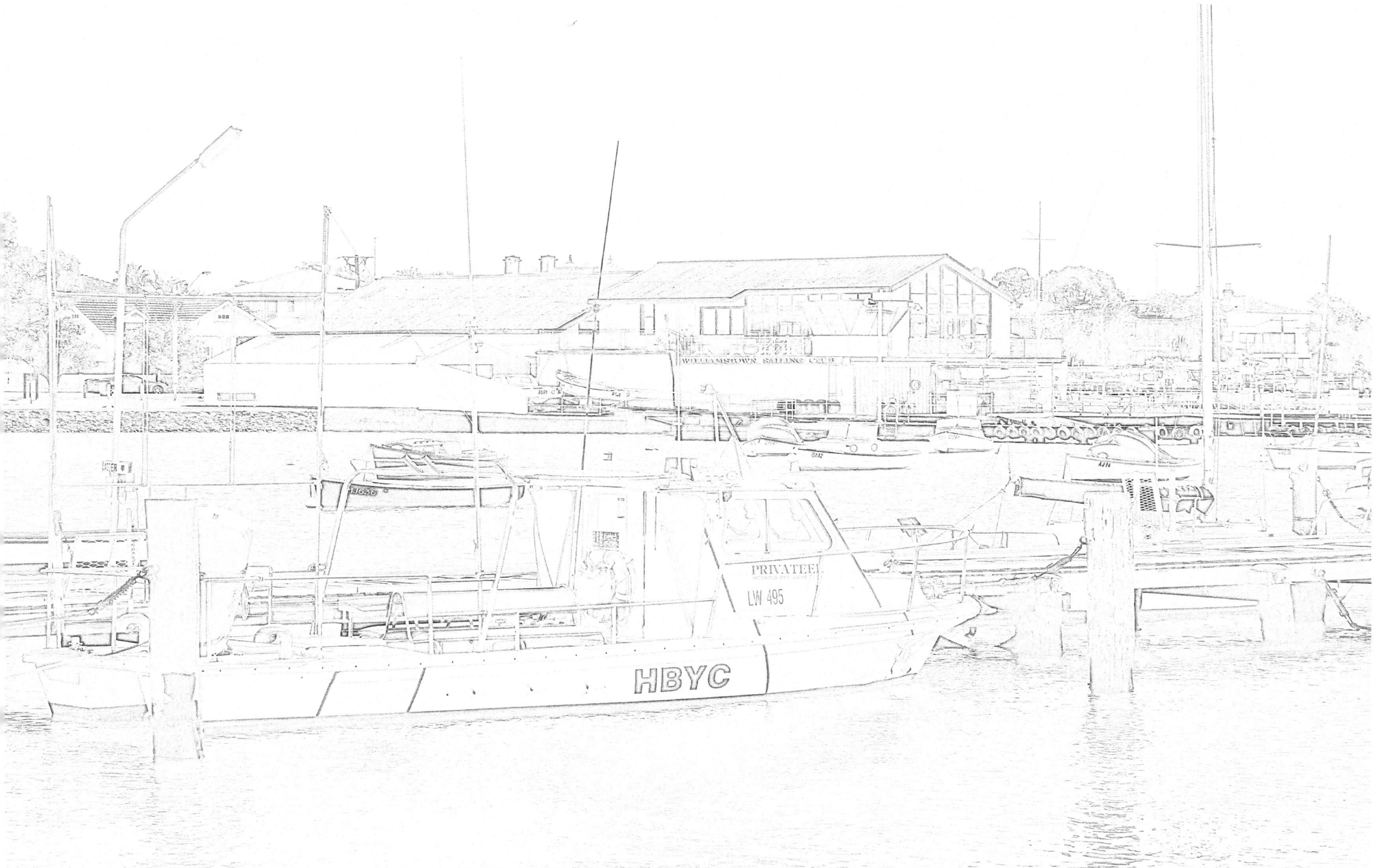
WILLIAMSTOWN SAILING CLUB
LW 495
HBYC

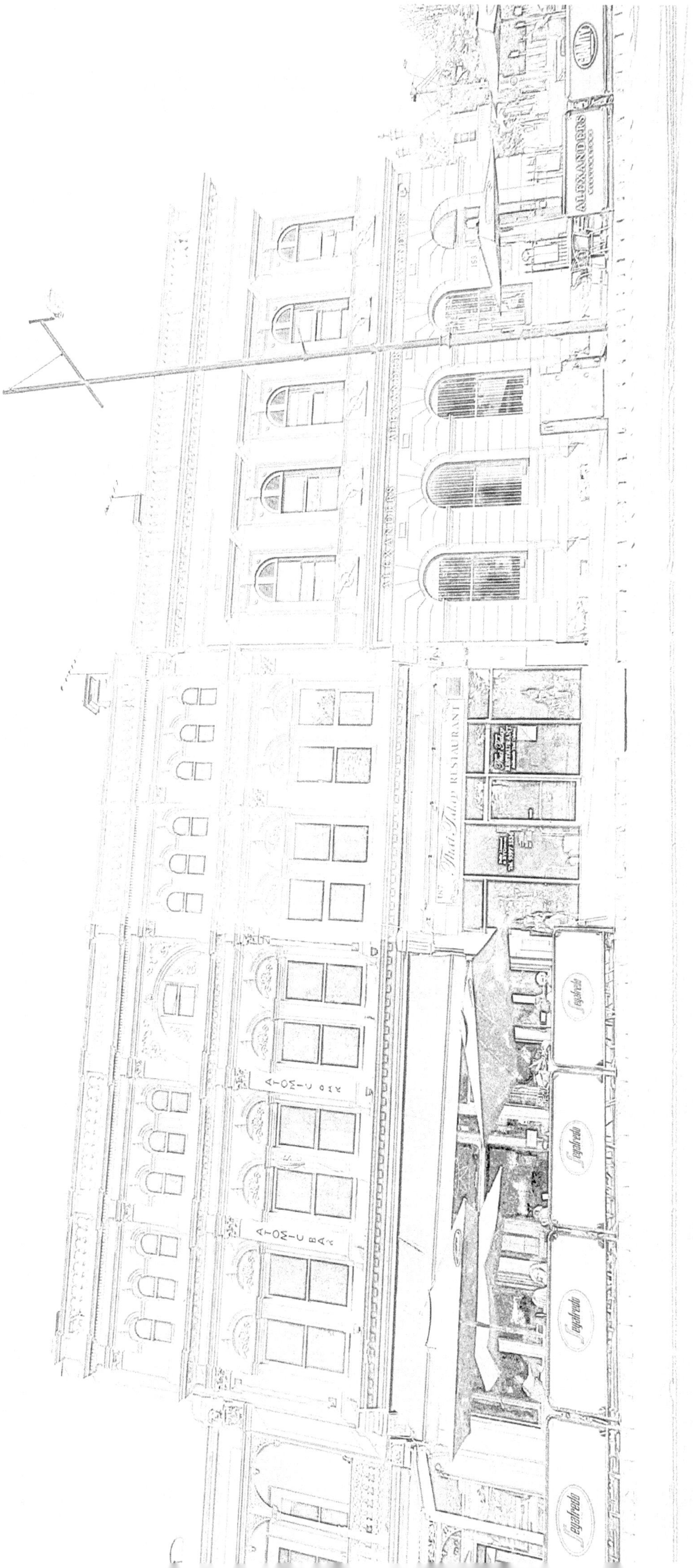
ALEXANDERS
RESTAURANT
ATOMIC BAR
Segafredo

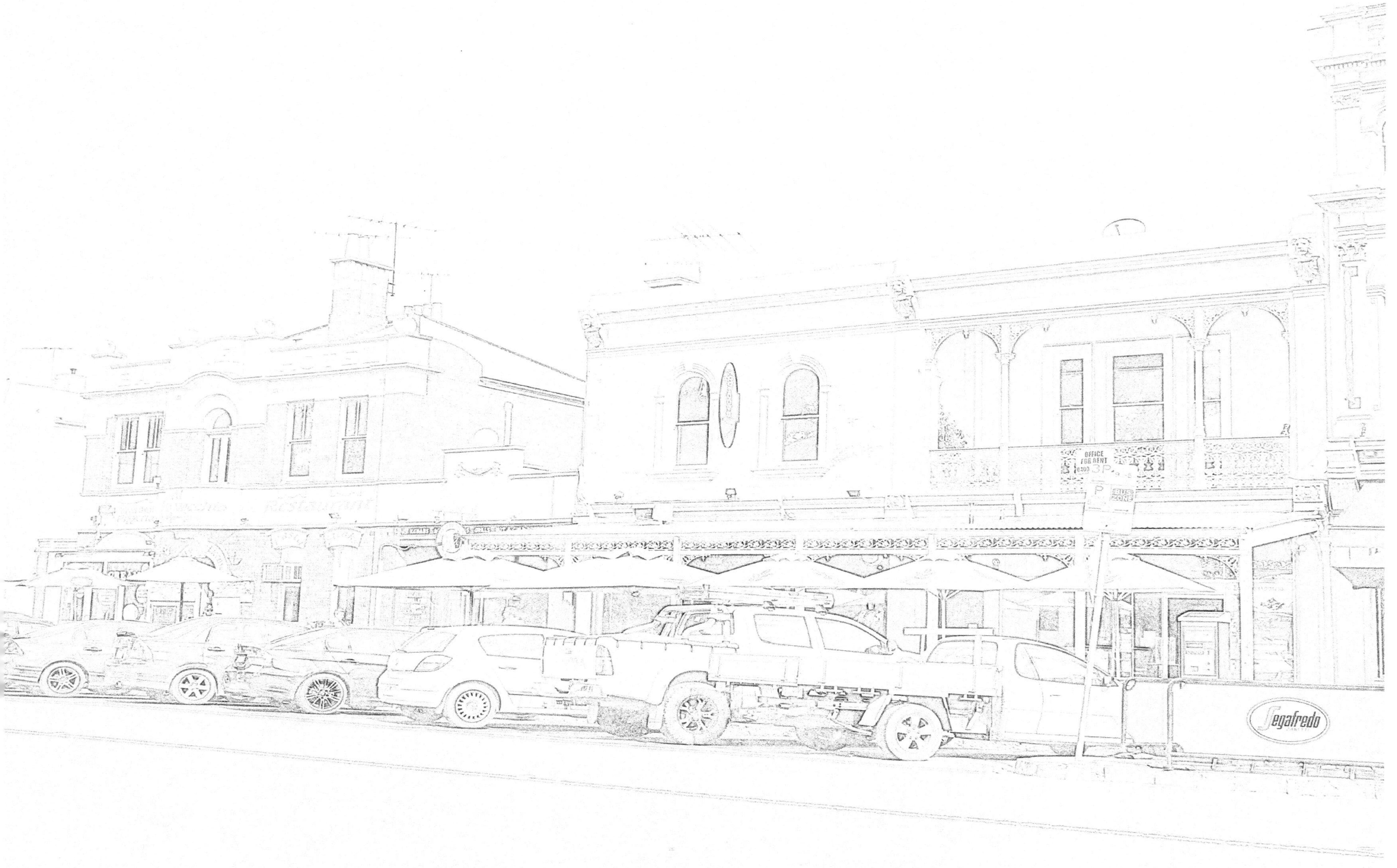
Restaurant
OFFICE FOR RENT
BUS ZONE
Segafredo

R.M.S. TITANIC LIVERPOOL
WHITE STAR LINE

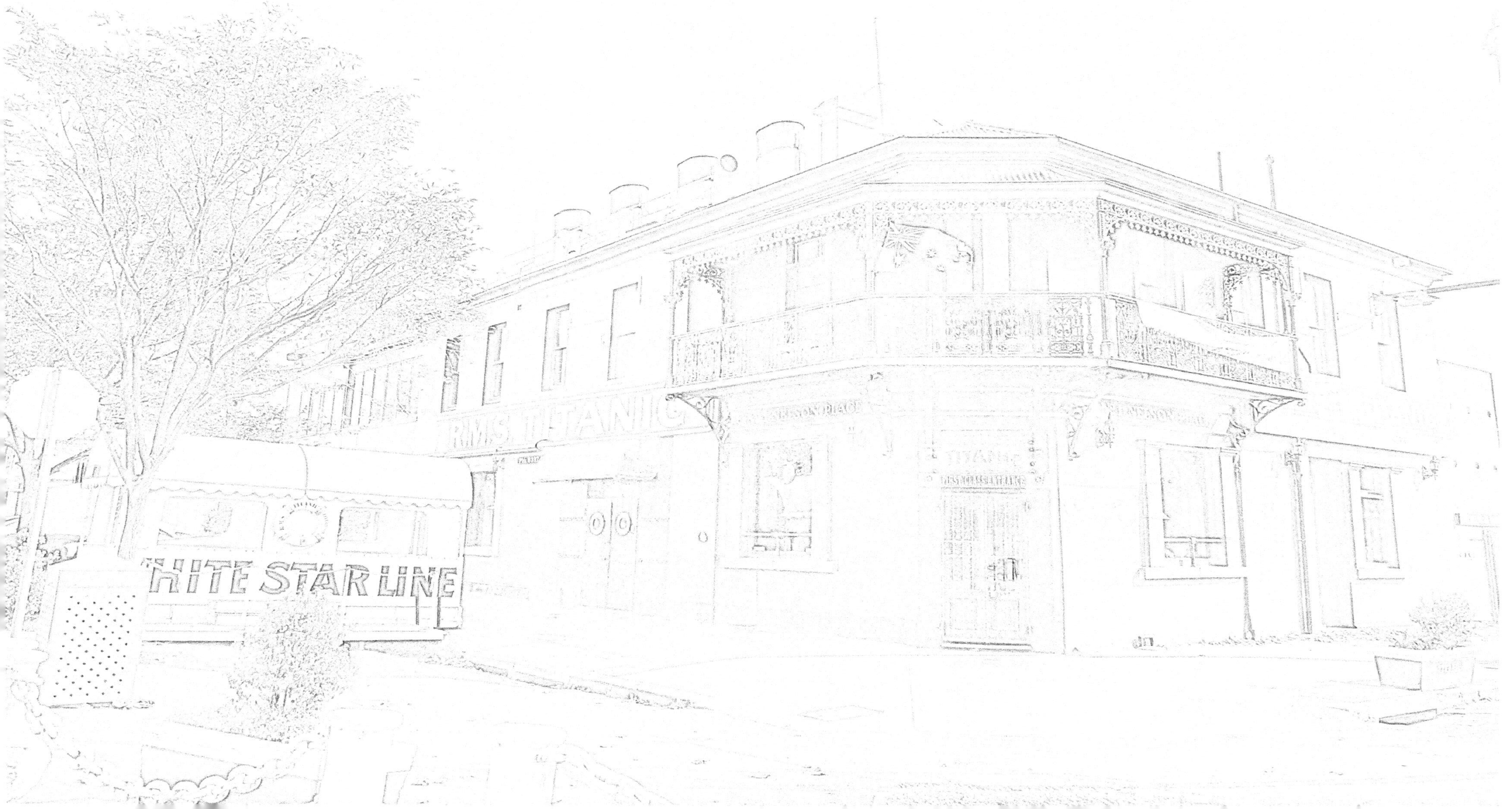
RMS TITANIC
HITE STAR LINE

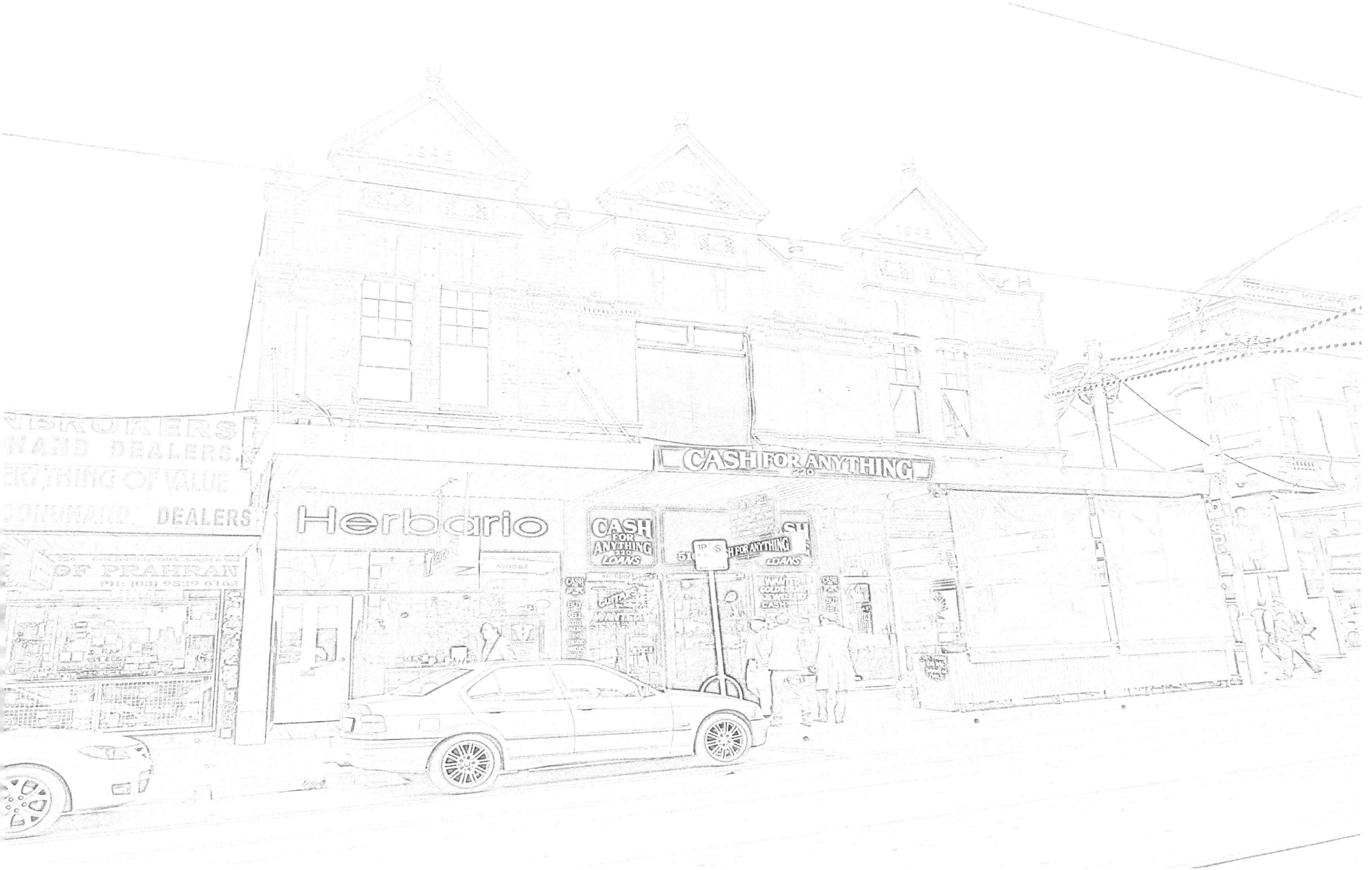
CASH FOR ANYTHING
220
Herbario
CASH FOR ANYTHING 220 LOANS
LOANS
DEALERS
PRAHRAN
PH: (03) 9529 6162

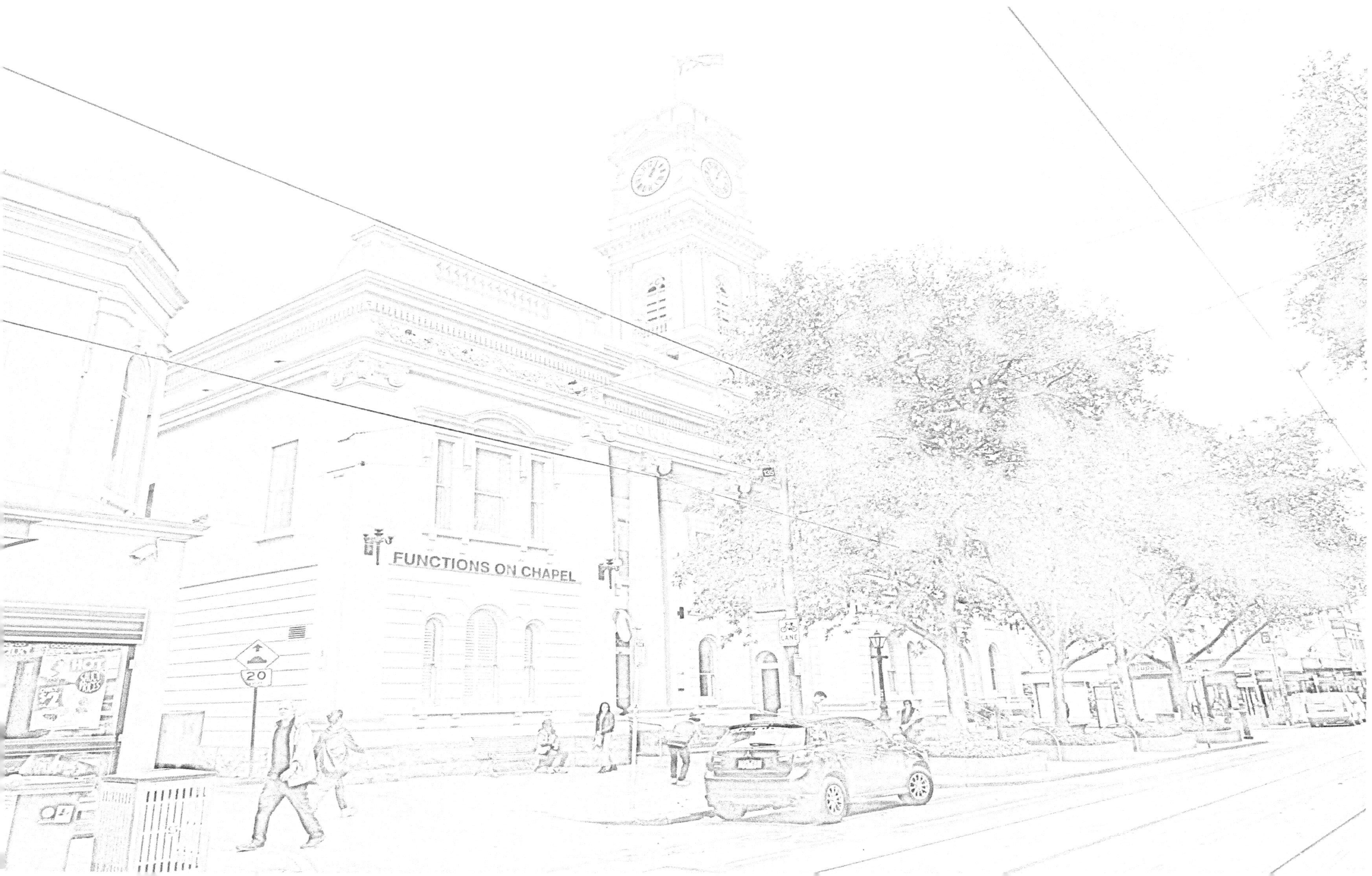
FUNCTIONS ON CHAPEL
20
LANE
HOT

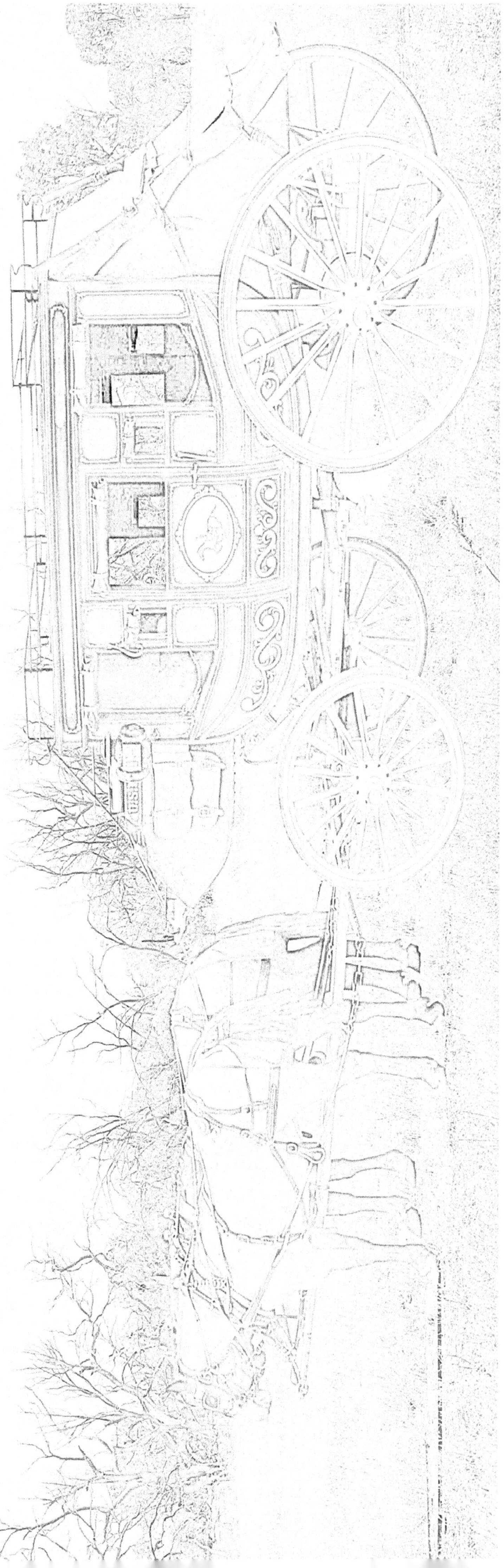

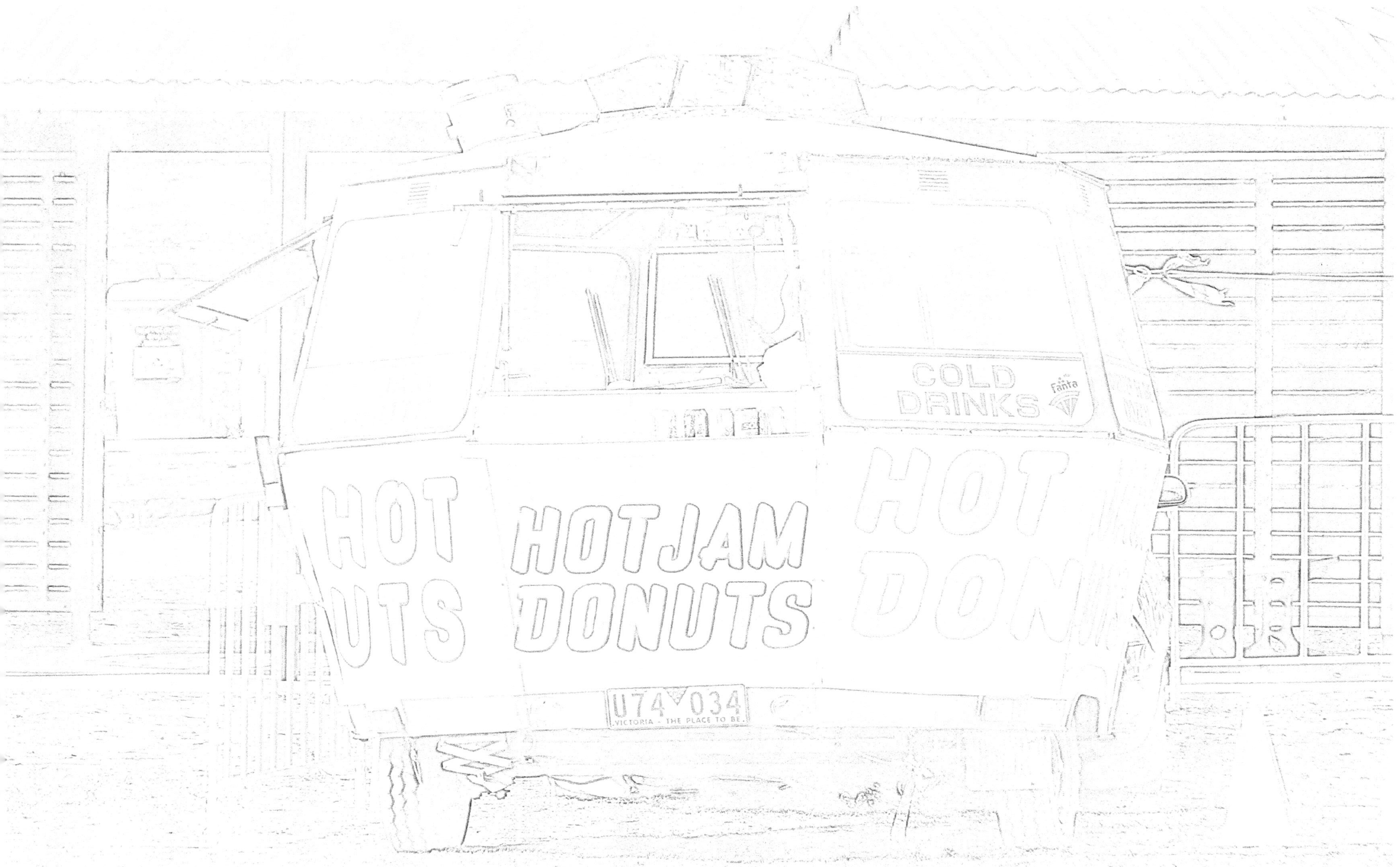
COLD DRINKS
Fanta
HOT
UTS
HOTJAM DONUTS
HOT
DON
U74 034
VICTORIA - THE PLACE TO BE

www.ingramcontent.com/pod-product-compliance
Lightning Source LLC
Chambersburg PA
CBHW081057180526
45170CB00005B/1785
* 9 7 8 0 3 5 9 8 6 4 7 9 9 *